Paris Hilton

Memoir

THE UNTOLD STORIES

William H Lemke

TABLE OF CONTENTS

PROLOGUE

CHAPTER 1: **BRIEF HISTORY OF MY PARTYING LEGACY**

CHAPTER 2: **IT ALL ADDS UP**

CHAPTER 3: **HEY, IT'S PARIS**

CHAPTER 4: **HE SAW IT. HE WANTED IT**

CHAPTER 5: **TOUGH LOVE**

CHAPTER 6: **LOCKED AWAY**

CHAPTER 7: **ESCAPE**

CHAPTER 8: **THE CASCADE SCHOOL**

CHAPTER 9: **THAT WAS SO ME**

CHAPTER 10: **THE FIRST STEP TO SELF-REINVENTION**

CHAPTER 11: **SMILE AT THE CAMERA**

CHAPTER 12: **HIT THE GROUND**

CHAPTER 13: **STARS ARE BLIND**

CHAPTER 14: **COACHELLA**

CHAPTER 15: **AMNESIA**

CHAPTER 16: **THIS IS PARIS**

PROLOGUE

Dr. Edward Hallowell, the author of Driven to Distraction, compares the ADHD brain to a Ferrari with bicycle brakes: strong yet difficult to control. My ADHD causes me to lose my phone, but it also shapes who I am, so if I want to enjoy my life, I must embrace my ADHD.

And I enjoy my life.

It's June 2022, and I am having one of my best weeks ever. My neighbor, Christina Aguilera, invited me to be one of her top-secret special guests at LA Pride, and as my crew moved my DJ equipment out the door, I was so nervous and excited that I left the house without my shoes and arrived at a backstage trailer in a tank top, velour track pants, and socks, which was made even more embarrassing when I accidentally went into the wrong dressing room. Some backup dancers were in there getting ready and yelled with delight when they saw me.

So, take selfies. Obviously.

I always try to do it myself—like hold the person's camera so it's angled down, which is important if you're tall, because it's so unflattering when the angle is up your nostrils or the person's hands are shaking because they're maybe nervous and a bit shy, which I totally relate to, so I did that with "Loves it! Loves it! Sliving!" and all the things, and then off I went in my socks, doing this thing my husband, Carter, calls the "unicorn trot": not fully running, more I have a hard time going slowly.

So then I'm there at Pride with Christina and about thirty thousand other people, all decked out in rainbows and sparkles, dancing, laughing, hugging, having the best time during my set, which came right after Kim Petras, who sang at our wedding last year—this beautiful ballad version of "Stars Are Blind" and then "Can't Help Falling in Love" as Carter and I walked down the aisle—which is why that song brought tears to my eyes last week at Britney Spears's wedding when our gorgeous angel princess bride emerged, after all those nightmare years, and floated down the aisle in Versace (because Versace, please) with that iconic Elvis Presley song, which has been sung at millions of weddings in Vegas, where my grandfather, Barron Hilton, started the whole Vegas residency trend by having Elvis at the Las Vegas Hilton International back in 1969, paving the way for Britney and so many other groundbreaking performers to flourish in that format, a perfect example of how one person's creative vision sparks a cascade of genius that goes on and on into the future.

Another fantastic example is my great-grandfather, Conrad Hilton.

Wait. Where was I?

Pride!

This crowd. Oh my God. Energy. Love. Light. Unbreakable spirit.

I am behind the board. It's like piloting a starship filled with the coolest individuals in the galaxy. My set is built around legendary music like "Toxic" as well as a great BeatBreaker remix of "Genie in a Bottle" by Xtina, Queen of the Night, and a slew of other dope originals and remixes, which I should post on the podcast or YouTube because this set is so much fun. (Note to self: Create a playlist for this book.) I was so concentrated on my set (note to self: add Ultra Naté to playlist) that I didn't realize until halfway through that I had left my phone on the counter in the trailer where I took selfies with the half-dressed backup dancers.

Fuck.

As an adult, I have been inconsistent with my medicine. When I was in my early twenties, a doctor described what was "wrong" with me and prescribed Adderall. I had a love/hate relationship with Adderall for approximately 20 years until Carter and I met with Dr. Hallowell.

Dr. Hallowell stated, "I've been trying to communicate to people since 1981 that this condition, when used appropriately, is an asset composed of attributes that cannot be purchased or taught. Stigma holds us back. Stigma plus ignorance. "A lethal combination."

I felt the lightning bolt you get when someone says a painful truth you've always known but have never heard said aloud.

"Our kryptonite is boredom," explained Dr. Hallowell. "If stimulus is not present, we manufacture it. "We self-medicate with adrenaline."

ADHD can be a source of creative energy, but it also has a negative side effect of being a troublemaker. Do you want some adrenaline? Do things the hard way. Get into a train wreck relationship. There are countless ways to screw yourself over for the sake of adrenaline. My imagination is limitless, but it takes me to dark regions as easily as it does to light. Dr. Hallowell refers to it as the Demon, a snake that slithers into everything, telling you that if it's awful, you deserve it, and if it's nice, it won't last. Of course, the Demon is a liar, but try explaining that to my brain, which is wanting a large bucket of deep-fried anxiety.

"Your greatest asset is your worst enemy," explained Dr. Hallowell.

And my brain said, "Fuck."

"Tell me, Paris, how is your self-esteem?"

"I'm good at pretending," I explained.

He continued: "That's common among people who live with ADHD."

Specifically, "people who suffer from ADHD." Specifically, "people afflicted with ADHD."

People with ADHD.

Some of us have realized that ADHD is our superpower. I wish the A represented ass-kicking. I wish the letters D meant for dope and drive. I wish the H had recommended heck yeah.

I'm not gloating or complaining; I'm simply telling you that this is my thinking. It has a lot to do with how this book is going to turn out, because I adore run-on sentences—and dashes. And sentence fragments. I'm probably going to jump around a lot while telling this narrative.

The Spirograph of Time. It's all connected.

I have avoided discussing some of these concerns for decades. I am an issue-avoiding machine. I learned from the best: my parents. Nicky describes Mom and Dad as "the king and queen of sweeping things under the rug."

There is a hierarchy, and the following are the rules in my family:

It's fine if you don't discuss anything.

If you disguise how badly you were hurt, it did not happen.

You don't have to feel awful if you appear to be unaware of how profoundly you hurt someone else.

Of course, that is just nonsense, and to make matters worse, it is bad business. I come from a family of talented businesses. How are we so lousy at emotional economics? Professional and personal relationships are based on transactions. Give and receive. For better or worse. You make an investment with the expectation of receiving a good return. But there is always risk.

I love my mother, and I know she loves me. Still, we've put each other through hell and can't say more than a few words about certain things. It will be difficult for her to read this book. I wouldn't be surprised if she kept it on a shelf for a while. Or forever. And that's fine.

I'm attempting to take ownership of some deeply personal issues that I've never been able to discuss. Things I have said and done. Things have been said and done to me. I have difficulty trusting others and am hesitant to disclose my intimate ideas. I'm really protective of my family and my brand—the businesswoman who developed out of a party girl and the party girl who still lives within the businesswoman—so it makes me nervous to think about what others may say.

But it's time.

There are numerous young women who need to hear this narrative. I do not want them to learn from my failures; instead, I want them to quit blaming themselves for their own mistakes. I want children to laugh and realize that they have a voice, their own brand of brilliance, and, girl, they don't have to fit in.

CHAPTER 1

BRIEF HISTORY OF MY PARTYING LEGACY

When I was younger, I primarily attended family events at Brooklawn, the house of my father's parents, Barron and Marilyn Hilton, whom I affectionately referred to as Papa and Nanu. You may have seen this property on my docuseries Paris in Love; it is the Georgian-style estate where I will marry in 2021. The mansion, designed by famed architect Paul R. Williams, who also designed residences for Frank Sinatra, Lucille Ball, Barbara Stanwyck, and other Hollywood icons, was erected in 1935 for Jay Paley, one of CBS's founders.

Papa was eight years old at the time, and he lived in a hotel with his older brother Nicky, younger brother Eric, and my great-grandfather Conrad Hilton. According to family mythology, my great-grandmother abandoned them because she disliked the hardworking hotel life and gave up hope that Conrad would ever have actual money. (Mentally inserting the "Bye, Felicia" gif.)

Conrad later had a brief marriage to Hungarian socialite Zsa Zsa Gabor, who was penniless but gorgeous and enjoyed going out dancing every night. Zsa Zsa had a vibrant personality and pioneered an early form of the influencing business model, which involved being paid to wear clothes, attend parties, and promote beauty goods in order for brand names to appear in the Hollywood press. Conrad's marriage ended bitterly, and he thought it was best to raise the boys himself. He raised them with old-school Christian principles, forcing them to work as bellhops and teaching them that work and family are jealous gods who will always battle for a man's time and undivided attention. Papa married Nanu after World War II, and they have eight children. Dad is ranked sixth. When he was a child, they moved into the Jay Paley home and called it Brooklawn.

All of this may appear to be old history, but in order to comprehend my story, you must first understand the Hilton. People who knew Conrad Hilton have told me that I am very similar to him, which I mainly take as a compliment. Mostly. He died two years before I was born, and, contrary to popular belief, he gave the majority of his fortune to charity. Papa worked. My parents worked. I'm a hardworking individual. In 2022, I signed a major contract to be the face of Hilton Hotels in ad campaigns and cross-promotions on my social media, and while I enjoy working with them, I believe that is the most money I'll ever make as a Hilton.

But I am a Hilton, and that is huge. Here I am, acknowledging my blessings and luck, okay? My family has been dubbed "American royalty." I'm not downplaying the incredible advantage or access that provided me. Experiences. Travel. Opportunities. I am grateful for all of it.

The Barron Hilton family is large, and we stick together, loving each other and minding each other's business, even if we haven't seen each other as much since Nanu died. Nicky and I used to spend our childhood days climbing fences and playing kickball on Brooklawn's gorgeous green lawn. Brooklawn parties were carnival-style, complete with pony rides, petting zoos, bouncy castles, tennis tournaments, and Marco Polo death bouts in the massive pool, which included an exquisite mosaic of imported Italian tile depicting the zodiac signs. I'm an Aquarius, so I assumed I'd be the one that looked like a mermaid, but it turned out to be Virgo. Aquarius appeared to be a muscular man carrying a water jug on his shoulder. I think I sobbed when I found out. Actually, I probably cried for about three seconds before deciding I was the mermaid, regardless of what the stars or some old Italian tile people claimed.

My parents, Rick and Kathy Hilton, spent the 1970s partying with

Andy Warhol and the most hippest audiences from Studio City to Studio 54. My father is a real estate and financial professional who cofounded Hilton & Hyland, a large firm that specializes in high-end corporate and residential real estate. My parents did a lot of entertaining for his business, and when Mom throws a party, she prepares everything down to the last rose petal, making her guests feel like they're a part of something special. Everything is perfect, even the hostess. My mother dresses herself and her surroundings with perfect elegance. She enters a party and works the room like a royal—savvy, kind, and stunning. People adore her because she actually cares about them, listens to them, and makes them feel intelligent, kind, and attractive.

True sophistication is the capacity to fit in anywhere because you understand and respect everyone. Mom is sophisticated like that. She's humorous, smart, and fashionable, but savvy is her true superpower. I had no idea how much ridiculous energy she had stored up inside her until she agreed to do The Real Housewives of Beverly Hills in 2021. It was as if somebody had popped the cork on a bottle of pink champagne.

Mom taught Nicky and me party etiquette when we were younger, before the brothers arrived. What fork to use. How to position our feet when standing for red carpet shots. We recognized that our family name carried weight and attracted attention. We had a specific position in society, which came with certain expectations. As small girls, Nicky and I attended ultra stylish social parties, fundraising events, holiday galas, and expensive receptions at the Waldorf or the Met, where my parents socialized with lawyers, agents, politicians, and all kinds of remarkable people who accomplished great things.

One of my earliest recollections is of sitting on Andy Warhol's knee and painting sketches during an after-party at the Waldorf-Astoria. He adored me and frequently told my mother, "This kid is going to be a huge star."

I adore how my parents included us in everything. You might assume that fancy business and social events would be boring for a young child, but I loved those parties. I came to appreciate the architecture of a beautiful ball gown. I was exposed to excellent music, including jazz combinations, string quartets, and private performances by notable performers. I sat like a butterfly on a fence, listening in on adult conversations about corporate machinations, real estate transactions, fortunes won and lost, ill-advised love affairs, and nasty divorces. It was all about love and money, which captivated me because everyone appeared to be obsessed with one or the other.

I was twelve years old when I first went to a club. Nicky and I were friends with Pia Zadora's daughter Kady, and Pia was friends with our mother, so we got to accompany her to a New Kids on the Block concert in Los Angeles. Because Pia was a celebrity, we were able to go backstage—and we were dying.

"We're going to Bar One for the after-party," the boys told Pia. "You should come."

Nicky, Kady, and I were like, "We have to go!" Please! Pleeeeeease!" We were all completely infatuated with New Kids. Pia was cool, so we headed to Bar One, where the bouncers allowed her in right away because she was a celebrity.

The atmosphere inside Bar One blew my little head. I had an immediate visceral response like yaaaasssss because—LIGHTS MUSIC! LAUGHTER FASHION MUSIC. JOY LIGHTS WHITE TEETH DIAMONDS MUSIC—a dose of the dazzling sensory input that my ADHD brain desired. I had no idea I was experiencing a genuine alteration in my body chemistry, but I knew I was feeling something real, and I liked it. Every aspect of me came alive—body, brain, skin, and spirit—and it felt amazing.

Unfortunately, just as I was taking it all in, we ran across my mother's sister. Aunt Kyle exclaimed, "WTF!" She dragged Pia aside for a quick, hissy discussion before taking us home, but I knew I had to go back.

In my early teens, I took advantage of each sneak-out opportunity I could find. I became one of the Desperately Seeking Susan club kids that ruled the nightlife scene in the early 1990s. The vogue dancers, drag queens, and Harajuku girls took me under their wing and looked out for me, which is how I learned the crucial ingredients of partying like a rockstar:

Stay hydrated.

Stay attractive (tipsy is cute, but drunk is disgusting).

Wear excellent, sturdy platform boots and comfy clothes so you can dance all night and easily climb in and out of windows and over fences if necessary.

I didn't drink or use drugs back then. When I was a youngster, joy was the only party drug I required. I was not there to get drunk; I was there to dance. Alcohol and drugs are used to escape reality, and I wanted to experience as much reality as possible. The escape from drinking did not occur until later.

Following the Pia Zadora club escapade, I attempted to smuggle Nicky, our cousin Farah, and our friend Khloé Kardashian into Bar One. Khloé and Farah were tiny middle school girls, so I dressed Khloé up in full makeup, a long red wig, and a floppy black hat.

I replied: "If anyone asks, your name is Betsey Johnson."

Farah sat on someone's shoulders, wearing a large trench coat. We put so much work into our disguises that we were surprised we didn't make it beyond the velvet rope.

"I guess you need to be with someone famous," I told you.

I didn't like feeling rejected in front of everyone. I was not going to let this happen again. When I was sixteen, I set up fake IDs for Nicky and myself. We weren't fooling anyone, but we were becoming somewhat well-known, so we had no trouble going into Bar One (now Bootsy Bellows), Roxbury (now Pink Taco), and other trendy spots.

My partying options were limited between the ages of sixteen and eighteen because I was incarcerated in a series of cult wilderness boot camps and "emotional-growth boarding schools." When I escaped for a few precious weeks of freedom, I kept it simple with tiny beach parties and living room gatherings where kids were just chilling and talking, until I forced everyone to get up and dance. Especially children who were overly bashful or self-conscious about their bodies. They're the ones who need to dance the most. This remains the rule at every gig I DJ, whether in the virtual or real world: When you party with Paris, you dance.

At the age of 18, I signed with a modeling agency. What do you think people want to do after a runway show? Party with models. It's easy to think, "No duh," but go past the simple idea that men are pigs and models are dumb. That is not fair, true, or useful. Most men, I believe, are generally decent, and successful models travel the world. Traveling the world is the most effective form of education. Most models are in their teens and twenties, and their lack of maturity can be noticeable at times, but they are maturing. Give them a minute.

Networking—knowing how to work a party—is an important part of expanding a business. In my twenties, I was so skilled at both partying and business that people began paying me to attend their parties. I did not invent getting paid to party; rather, I reinvented it. I'm proud to be known as the original influencer. Girls must appreciate the importance they offer to the party. It's much more than just standing around looking lovely. Mannequins can do this. A successful party girl is a facilitator, negotiator, and diplomat—she's the sparkler and matchmaker.

Know your worth, ladies. You aren't lucky to be at the party; the party is fortunate to have you. Apply as needed in relationships, jobs, and family.

My twenty-first birthday in 2002, like my wedding in 2021, took place over several days and time zones. I'd been going to clubs for years, but I was tired of bullshitting bouncers and passing off bogus IDs—as if they didn't know. It turned us all into pretenders, which seems like a waste of energy. I was excited to turn twenty-one and leave everything behind. This was my first time going out all nice and legal, so I went big, preparing parties all over the world and arranging for sponsors to pay for everything. My coming-of-age party was a dancing, drinking, and hobnobbing marathon that left folks exhausted.

Obviously, I put together outstanding clothing. This was a multi-look event with a wide range of design-forward dresses, platform shoes, accessories, and diamond tiaras. This was the inspiration behind my iconic silver chain-mail dress by Julien Macdonald, which Kendall Jenner duplicated for her own twenty-first birthday celebration in 2016. That demonstrates how ageless this dress is. I wore mine again (yep, I saved it!) on my final night in Marbella, Spain, where I was DJing in 2017.

Julien made me the chain-mail outfit for my London party at the end of London Fashion Week, when I also walked in his show. I was the bride, and the bride's attire was stunning, but the first time I set eyes on that classic chain-mail birthday dress, I was completely taken aback.

"This dress is everything," I explained. "This dress is going to end up in a museum someday."

The weight and construction are finely designed, with thousands of

Swarovski crystals. It behaves like a liquid Slinky. The neckline is cut all the way down to Argentina, requiring double-sided tape to avoid nip slip. That normally works great until you break a sweat on the dance floor, but dancing in that dress is preferable to a milk bath.

I had fallen on my face while running to hug someone, so I decided to take off my six-inch heels. I believe that's when I changed into my floating blue mermaid dress. Backless, yet well-built. At the GO Lounge in Los Angeles, I donned a sheer pink mini studded with trillions of hand-sewn diamante beads. But nothing made me feel as good as dancing my ass off that night in London's Stork Lounge in that silver Julien Macdonald dress.

I want every girl to feel this way on her twenty-first birthday: free, happy, gorgeous, and loved.

Invincible.

CHAPTER 2

IT ALL ADDS UP

I was born in New York City on February 17, 1981, three days after Valentine's Day: Aquarius sun, Leo moon, and Sagittarius rising. Six months later, MTV made its official debut with the Buggles' song "Video Killed the Radio Star."

In the context of a technological renaissance, my life narrative makes complete sense.

Everyone claims I was a sweet child. My parents have hundreds of hours of home footage to back this up. My father was always an early user of technology, and as soon as those huge old-school camcorders became available, he bought one and embraced the idea that everything should be documented, for pleasure now and historical value later. He recorded my entire existence, beginning with the day I was born. I enjoyed the sense of his fixed gaze on me. In those moments, his focus was drawn to that small round lens, and I was in the center of it.

Dad always referred to me as "Star"—not only in the sense of "movie star," but also in the sense of "I wonder what you are."

My younger sister Nicholai Olivia was born when I was two years old, and Cyndi Lauper released her first hit, "Girls Just Want to Have Fun". Aunt Kyle claims I was over the moon, madly in love with Nicky from the day she arrived home. I have no memory of a life before her. She was my childhood best friend and crime partner. Mom clothed us in twin outfits. We dressed up in Mom's wardrobe, dressing each other with scarves and jewels and sashaying down a make-believe runway.

I've been dragging Nicky on excursions and escapades ever since. I relied on Nicky to support me if I was doing something out of limits, such as hiding a ferret in a box beneath my bed or climbing out my upper bedroom window and tumbling down the trellis when I was grounded. She's been attempting to put the brakes on me since she was old enough to understand the term repercussions. When she was in junior high, she became a little tattle-tale, but I believe she honestly thought she was watching out for me.

My brain skipped and flashed with the chemical imbalance caused by ADHD since I was a toddler. Sometimes it was too much. I had to get up and dance under the illumination of my Disney princess night light. "Time out" and anything else that required sitting motionless was tormenting me. I'm sure I was a handful, but lying and being rude were not in my nature. Nicky and I attended etiquette classes, so I knew how to apologize like a good girl and had enough practice. Being a "good girl" requires you to stay quiet.

Obey.

Sit still.

I was incapable of doing these things, so I had to be adorable instead. I needed to be sweet, precocious, and coy. I had to act goofy and use a baby-girl voice, which came naturally when I was frightened, because strain in your neck and shoulders restricts your vocal apparatus, causing your voice to sound high and glottal. (I learned this during vocal training for Repo! The Genetic Opera.) I sang, danced, and put on concerts in Nanu's living room with Nicky and our cats, but I was not interested in performing in front of others. Fundamentally, I've always been shy—an extroverted introvert who compensates with theatrical social butterfly behavior.

When Nicky and I were preschoolers, our family moved to Bel Air and into a house that my dad purchased from Jaclyn Smith of Charlie's Angels. Jaclyn had created an extravagant playhouse for her daughter, similar to Barbie's Dream House, which Nicky and I transformed into a pet motel. I always saved up money to go shopping for animals at a dank-smelling pet store that featured tropical fish, snakes, and other wonderful critters. I wanted to adore and comfort every small thing that came my way.

Nicky and I performed intricate dress-up and pretend games while Aunt Kyle photographed and filmed us with her video camera. Mom has only made a small portion of that footage available to the public. On one old home video, there's a telling moment where my eight-year-old face is all crooked smile and smeared lipstick, my bangs are straight out of "Forever Your Girl"—teased ragged with the appropriate hat—and I'm wearing Boy George blue eyeshadow and layers of bunchy, jewel-toned clothes typical of the late 1980s.

My father traveled extensively for business, and my parents do not sleep apart. She still follows him wherever he goes. So we traveled a lot as a family, or Mom would go with Dad while Aunt Kyle looked after us, which was fantastic since Kyle always pushed Nicky and me to invite friends around. There were a number of sleepovers with Nicole, my middle school best friend. We thought we were edgy because we knew every lyric to Sir Mix-a-Lot's "Baby Got Back."

Mom, Kim, and Kyle demonstrated an excellent model for sisterhood dynamics. Mom now tells me that their mother was extremely severe when she was a child, but Grandma appears to have relaxed slightly after divorcing my mother's father and marrying her second husband. Kim arrived five years later, and Kyle was born five years after that. Grandma divorced that guy, then married and divorced twice more, so those girls went through a lot as children, but they emerged with beauty, business acumen, great elegance, and a natural joie de vivre that I've always adored. They unconditionally supported, defended, and loved each other, but they could trust each other to tell the truth.

If one of them had broccoli in her teeth, the other two would alert her. Their energetic chats were always full of humor and confidence. Mom enjoys cracking people up.

One night, I strolled by my mother's chamber and heard her speak in an exaggerated little puppet voice. Kim and Kyle were laughing so hard they were almost sobbing. I don't remember the exact words, but I heard something like, "Nicole believes I should just approach him and tell him I think he's hot. Kim suggests I tell one of his buddies that I like him and see what happens.

It took a minute to settle in. She was reading from my BeDazzled diary.

I was too enraged to move. I stood behind the door, paralyzed, indignant, and humiliated. My aunts' laughter was not mean-spirited; they simply thought it was cute. And I'm sure it was really cute. I'm sure Mom just wanted to share this adorable thing with her sisters. After she went through my sock drawer. And read my diary. In a lamb chop puppet voice.

In terms of awful things that happen to children, this is not a major concern. I understand that. I'm merely noting it because the experience has lingered with me for a while. As when a glass slips from your grasp and shatters in the sink. In the grand scheme of things, it's not a big problem, but in that moment, you realize how fragile things are, and it makes you feel strangely frail yourself.

I'm not sure what happened to my diary. I wished I still had it. I think if I saw it, I'd chuckle too. But I'd also understand that it was beautiful. Sometimes we forget what it is to be a creative soul in that fleeting moment before being self-conscious and admitting that, yes, you do care what other people think of you. Especially those you love and admire.

My baby brother Conrad Hughes Hilton was born in 1994 when I was thirteen years old. I began paying more attention to music and clothes. I adored Madonna and Janet Jackson. I couldn't understand half of the lyrics in Salt-N-Pepa's "Shoop," but I could lip-sync to most of Da Brat's "Funkdafied" and Snoop Dogg's "Gin and Juice."

On New Year's Eve, my family, Nicole's family, and a group of other individuals we knew traveled to Vegas. My parents like Vegas, so this gathering was a longstanding tradition for all of us. Typically, the adults went out to dance in the New Year, while the children played board games and watched movies in their hotel suites with nannies. But that year, Nicole and I begged for our own rooms. We lobbied strongly, emphasizing how demeaning it was to be babysat at our senior age.

"We are teenagers! "We are old enough to babysit each other."

We finally convinced our parents that if they allowed us to stay in our own hotel room, we'd watch Dick Clark's New Year's Rockin' Eve and go to bed just after midnight.

Obviously, that did not happen.

By nine o'clock, we were bored and conversing on the phone with two Buckley boys who were a little older than us. Happy coincidence! They were in Vegas with their families, too. The boys came over to our hotel room and suggested we all go for a walk. Nicole and I had been forbidden to leave that room, but we wanted to be cool, so we claimed we could only stroll around the hotel for a little time, but then it seemed like we should avoid bumping into our parents, so the obvious decision was to walk down the Strip with the boys.

This was a lot of fun. We weren't attempting to drink or smoke; we just wanted to be where the action was. Music spilled from every entrance. People dressed in dazzling outfits and party hats to celebrate their happiness and beauty. At midnight, the street was filled with lights, jubilant crowds, and honking car horns. We made out with the boys—nothing more than first base—and then they left to do their own thing.

Nicole and I kept strolling on our own. We strolled and walked, taking everything in, window shopping, laughing, and speaking. People flooded out of casinos and hotel bars, in large numbers, to attend after-parties. It was overcrowded and a little scary. Nicole and I kept walking, arms clasped so we wouldn't be separated.

Finally, I replied, "We should get a cab and return to the hotel."

Nicole agreed, but everyone else on the street had the same thought. This was long before the advent of Uber and Lyft. You called a cab on a street corner or stood in line outside a hotel, but there were so many people that you couldn't even see a cab, let alone get inside one. Eventually, we approached a police officer who appeared busy but nice.

"Excuse me," I said. "Is there someplace we can catch a cab? There are about a million people waiting in line.

The cop focused his light on me and said, "How old are you?"

"Twenty-one." We did not skip a beat.

He folded his arms. "Show me your ID."

"I don't have it with me," I said. "I lost it."

"What's your name?"

"Jennifer Pearlstein," I announced. "This is my friend Leslie."

"How old are you, Jennifer?"

I told you! Twenty-one!"

"No, you're not."

"Eighteen?"

"You are not eighteen," he replied, "and it is illegal for you to be out on the Strip after nine." There is a curfew. You want to be arrested? "I should arrest you right now."

Nicole and I claimed that we were just eighteen and in town for business, but the cop wouldn't have it. He ordered us into the back of the cop cruiser, and we sat there like, "Holy crap!" What do we do? What do we do? While standing on the corner, he spoke into his shoulder radio.

We waited a long time. It seemed like two hours, but it was probably just fifteen minutes in real time. Nicole and I talked back and forth, getting our stories straight and devising a strategy. When the cop opened the car door, Nicole shouted out, "Her name is Paris Hilton!" We are staying at the Las Vegas Hilton! Her mother is Kathy Hilton!"

"Nicole." I elbowed her. "Oh, my god."

"We're very sorry, officer. "We didn't mean to do anything wrong," Nicole explained. She gave him my mother's phone number, and a short while later, my father arrived to get us. As expected, he raged at us the entire way back to the hotel.

"What were you thinking?" Do you have any ideas what might have happened? Star, you're grounded. Grounded!"

I was like, "Grounded from what? "I am already in Las Vegas."

"Grounded from Nicole," Dad remarked. "Obviously, you two are a horrible influence on one other. You are no longer permitted to hang out.

Nicole's parents were exactly as upset as mine, so it was double problems. They put us in different rooms and warned us not to talk to each other. When we returned to LA, our mothers confiscated the phones in our rooms, but Nicole's house was across the golf course from mine, and we learned that if we screamed from our balconies, it echoed across the green, allowing us to hear each other.

Love will find a way. There was no separating us.

Nicole Richie and I were ride-or-die during our terrible twos, and we'll be that way until the world dies. Everyone around us was dying while we were teenagers, riffing on each other and making funny sounds. We were dying. I am dying just thinking about it! I'm not sure what it was, but we seemed to resonate like tuning forks. We were having so much fun that a sort of Lucy and Ethel comedic magic occurred, which was the charm of The Simple Life.

Nicole is so genuinely lovely and sweet that her bawdy one-liners catch people off guard, and the reactions she receives are hilarious. Comedy must be daring, and Nicole does not hesitate.

One of our favorite hobbies was making prank calls, which we learned from my mother, the prank-calling GOAT. Mom can change her voice and make you believe a delivery person is on his way over with a hundred Hawaiian pizzas, that she is stuck in the trunk of her car, or absolutely anything. She and Nicky once took me to lunch at a small vineyard and pretended I was attending a surprise wedding where I was the bride.

Nicole and I spent hours in my room, inspired by Mom's spectacular prank-calling example, answering want ads in the Los Angeles Times or dialing boys from our class and pretending to be the appointment secretary for a professional sports scout. These calls usually went down similarly to the ones Nicole and I made using random numbers obtained on a bulletin board in a laundromat while filming The Simple Life.

CHAPTER 3

HEY, IT'S PARIS

I turned fourteen in February 1995. I adored Toy Story and Jumanji, as well as leaping up and down with one arm in the air, singing along to Montell Jordan's "This Is How We Do It." I was in eighth grade at a Catholic school. We wore boxy basics, but Nicky and I devised methods to reduce the skirts and customize them to our liking with Hello Kitty trinkets, smart shirt-tucking techniques, and blown-out hair. I couldn't wait to come home and kick that plaid skirt and stiff shirt to the corner. I ran around in surfboard shorts, big tees, and sneakers. I slept in boxers and baseball shirts that I took from Dad's clean clothes.

I was a tomboy, but I certainly didn't consider myself a child. I had a beeper and my own phone line, which was linked to my own answering machine. I repeatedly recorded the answering machine message, attempting to make my voice raspy and enticing like the phone sex lines promoted on late night television.

In the evening, I laid on my bed, chattering with my pals about extremely grown-up topics like whether Rachel and Ross from pals would ever get together and what was going on in after-school reruns of Beverly Hills, 90210.

Shannen Doherty was the bad girl icon of the mid-1990s. You couldn't go grocery shopping or buy candies from the newsstand without seeing her in the newspapers. She posed nearly naked for Playboy. She partied with boys, argued with girls, and then—unforgivable!—left the show. The same audience that helped her become the show's breakout star turned on her, and we all went with it: "What a slut. "What a bitch." All the banal comments made about the girl everyone loves after she transforms into the girl they love to loathe.

Mom had her hands full with the boys, so my messes, pets, and jumping around were starting to grate on her nerves. We'd always been close, but suddenly we were experiencing some of the friction burn that naturally occurs between mothers and teenage daughters. Mom was really conservative, whereas I was extremely not. I played Onyx's Bacdafucup on repeat and donned Gadzooks' obscene message tees. I talked out and didn't send thank-you notes, and anytime I wanted to dodge the maze of parental permits, I went out my bedroom window and slid down to the earth like Super Mario. The nuns grumbled about my school-day fidgeting, shit-disturbing, and lack of concentration.

I was frequently grounded, so my answer was to sneak out. Nicole and I once devised a scheme to attend a school dance that we were supposed to be grounded from due to our general misbehavior. We went to Judy's in Beverly Center and purchased two outfits: velvet shorts with crop tops and fishnets. (Not in excellent taste, but not completely improper. You saw hotter outfits on Dance Moms. Then we went to her father's house under the guise of working on a school assignment or something, put on the clothes, and layered baggy pants and jackets over them. We went to the dance, and both sets of parents thought we were at the other person's house.

We got a kick out of something like that.

The planning! The intrigue!

We never did anything bad; we just enjoyed feeling free and outwitting everyone who we thought was trying to hold us back. We were almost always caught and grounded again, which seemed incredibly harsh to us at the time. We were only investigating. What's it like to feel sexy? What does "sexy" even mean? These are very acceptable questions for teenage females to investigate.

However, it is troublesome when girls enter the exploration phase feeling secretive and ill-informed. If you transmit the message, "We don't talk about such things," your children will grow up believing that being an adult implies keeping secrets. The nuns did not teach us about reproductive health in biology class. We surely did not discuss Lolita in English class. Mom did not discuss amorphous concepts such as "private" and "dirty." I learnt the fundamentals from feminine hygiene advertisements in Seventeen. My concept of sexuality was a fog machine of Madonna videos, Calvin Klein ads, and a vaguely mischievous inclination that caused me to feel the same sting of guilt as when I stole a tube of lip gloss from Mom's purse.

So, with middle school graduation approaching, I felt like I was already in high school. Which indicates you're an adult, right? When the yearbook came out, all of the eighth graders were portrayed in their caps and gowns, with my photo titled "Finest Girl."

Isn't that another fantastic word? Like, "You're doing well. "You're fine." Or, "There's nothing wrong with this little girl." "She is fine!" Or perhaps fine and fragile, like a dragonfly wing?

However, this is definitely fine, much like hot. Like sexy. I was the sexiest eighth-grade girl! Because "sexy eighth grader" is a thing, right?

Like a Halloween costume?

I was satisfied with becoming the "Finest Girl." I leaned toward it.

Meanwhile, all the females in my class had a crush on this attractive young teacher. He was constantly extolling his physical attractiveness. Very Abercrombie. Hair is tousled. Penetrating eyes. Everyone adored him, even the nuns.

But he chose me. The Best Girl.

"I've got a crush on you," he admitted, flashing a seductive smile.

He made me feel significant and mature. He complimented and mocked me, claiming that all the other girls were gossiping about me behind my back because they were jealous. Jealous of my attractiveness. Because their partners probably wanted to break up with them the moment I entered the room. He asked for my private phone number and warned me not to disclose it to anyone.

"It's our secret," he said, and I guarded it like candy beneath my pillow. I never felt manipulated. I felt as if I were being adored. I was Marilyn Monroe waiting to happen. He couldn't change how he felt since I had cast my spell on him.

Why wouldn't I adore this story? It was all about me, the beautiful little me. The emphasis was on my alluring looks rather than his inappropriate actions.

Mr. Abercrombie contacted me virtually every night, and we spent hours discussing how mature, attractive, and clever I was, as well as how sensual, misunderstood, and unique I was. He reminded me that Princess Diana was 13 years younger than Prince Charles. And Priscilla Presley was my age when Elvis fell for her. I deserved a rock star. I deserved a prince. Because I was a princess. I deserved to be appreciated and loved in ways that eighth-grade males are unaware of.

Mr. Abercrombie convinced me that I was unusual and precious, and you know what? I was. Each eighth-grade girl is unique and valuable. Every eighth-grade girl is a gem, like a priceless work of art, and you'd like to believe that every eighth-grade teacher will act like a security guard in an art gallery. He isn't there to enjoy the beauty; he's there to preserve it. He is there to police the regulations, and Rule Number One is: DO NOT TOUCH. Keep your fingers, lips, and man bits away from the artworks. It should be evident that the Girl with a Pearl Earring deserves to be able to smile her forlorn grin without some creepy person feeling her up. Because harm to a valuable work of art can be concealed, but it cannot be repaired.

My teacher would question me almost every night, "Are your parents home?"

One night, while they were away, I said, "No, it's just the nanny."

"Come outside," he instructed. "I'm waiting for you."

I put on my sneakers, went out my bedroom window, and slid down the drain pipe. My lungs were full with night air and the scent of mown grass and gardenias. I noticed a late-model SUV idling at the top of the driveway. I got into the passenger seat. Teacher took me into his arms and kissed me.

The intensity of it astounded and exhilarated me. My mind erupted, filled with adrenaline, curiosity, and a slew of other emotions I couldn't put into words. This terrified blissful kissing lasted for what felt like a long time and appeared to be growing into something else. I'm not sure where he would have gone if my parents hadn't pulled in the driveway.

Headlights streamed across the windshield, breaking the trance.

I caught a glimpse of my father's astonished expression. The teacher inserted his key into the ignition and ripped it out. As we fishtailed down the driveway, I grasped the edge of my seat. He drove like a crazy through the wealthy streets of Bel Air and Westwood, spinning around bends and flipping out the entire time.

I giggled. Nervous. Heart is throbbing. Ears are ringing. Oh my God! I wasn't wearing my seatbelt! It was like Bonnie and Clyde!

"Fuck! Fuck! Fuck!" Mr. Abercrombie sounded like he was crying. "My life is over. What Am I doing? "Why did you make me do this?"

He eventually came back and left me off in front of my house. He didn't even kiss me good night, like I expected from a date. It wasn't like a romantic comedy; he just dumped me out of the car and drove away. I dashed across the yard, scrambled up the drainpipe, climbed through the bedroom window, and got beneath the covers. My parents stormed into my room, enraged, screaming at me. There were too many words to sort through. A solid wall of fury.

I blinked my huge eyes and asked in a dreamy baby voice, "What?" What exactly are you talking about? "I have been sleeping."

I wasn't sure what else to do. I'm sure they didn't believe me for a second, but whatever—I just wanted them to leave, and they obviously wanted to leave, so they walked out of my room, and no one addressed the unpleasant episode ever again.

The school year was almost over, but the final month or two had been filled with drama at both school and home. I never told anyone, yet it seemed like everyone knew. Perhaps I imagined it, but something felt different. He remained Mr. Abercrombie, but I was no longer the Finest Girl. I was the Catholic School's Shannen Doherty. Everyone liked to despise me. Nothing I did was correct. I had no idea how to feel or what to do, and I was trying to digest it all in the lonely, perplexing confines of secret.

During the school dance following the graduation ceremony, I went to McDonald's, but when I returned, the chaperones refused to let me in.

The nuns exclaimed, "You're done, bitch. GTFO."

They probably didn't use those exact words, but they were apparent. I had to contact my mother to come fetch me, knowing she would be furious and embarrassed.

That was the end of my joyful days in Barbie's Bel Air Dream

House.

Mom and Dad sent me to live with my grandma in Palm Springs for the summer, which turned out to be much longer.

I'm not sure if there were any consequences for the teacher or if anyone tried to stop him from choosing another little child. My parents never gave me any information, and I never asked, but I believe the fear of negative publicity would have kept them from making a disturbance or filing charges. I understand how they could have concluded that this was in my best interests.

CHAPTER 4

HE SAW IT. HE WANTED IT

My family had moved into a sick apartment at the Waldorf while I was in Palm Springs with Gram Cracker, and I was really jealous. How can I not be? You must understand that this was not like a hotel room or even a hotel suite. This was a 2,500-square-foot condo with Italian marble, art deco architectural elements, magnificent light fixtures, and city vistas from every angle, including the bathtub.

It was a little hard at first, trying to fit in with the home rhythm, which was very different from our previous laid-back California household. Everyone was doing their own thing, and I didn't have a clear "thing" straight away. Mom had made a lovely room for me with white linens, a fluffy pink rug, and all of the dolls and plush animals I adored as a child. The only difficulty was that I was no longer a child. A lot had transpired. I am fifteen now. In high school. I had my own views about what I wanted my life and personal space to be like, but I largely kept them to myself. I didn't want to appear ungrateful, but I was quite appreciative!

So. Damn. GRATEFUL.

I am grateful to be home.

I am grateful to be loved.

I'm grateful for the family sounds around me.

My lovely siblings—I adored them. I adored watching cartoons with my younger brothers, who bounced about and climbed on me. I enjoyed racing about the hotel with my younger sister, who swiped my clothes and attempted to order me around. I adored my parents, who were always busy with exciting things while still finding time to chastise me about education, politeness, and blah blah blah. I am not being ironic here. I was overjoyed to be back in the embrace of my wonderfully flawed family. I would not have altered anything about them. I was like, "Wheeeeeeeeeeeee!" "Thank you, God."

Believe me, I was well aware of how wonderful and fortunate I was.

The entire neighborhood was buzzing with activity and excitement both day and night. Nicky and I occasionally dressed up and invited ourselves to parties. Or we'd sneak into an empty ballroom after a major event, running around in our PJs and bare feet, rummaging through the elegant dessert carts and checking out the leftover gifts. It was Candyland for two adolescent females who were increasingly infatuated with fashion, music, and art.

That summer, we took a vacation to the Hamptons, which seemed like another homecoming for me. I was in a familiar place with my loved ones. Guys began hitting on me and telling me I should be a model, which is something guys say, so who cares, but back in New York, the individuals who said Nicky and I should model were legitimate in that industry. Agents. Designers. Photographers. We discovered we could make money on our own.

"Absolutely not," Mom replied. "Not until you're eighteen."

Nicky always has a level head in situations like this, so I let her do the majority of the talking.

"You and Dad were just telling us in the Hamptons that we should get a job," she recalled.

"We meant babysitting," Mom said. "Working in an ice cream shop. "Something like that."

"Mom," Nicky replied, "you were modeling when you were a little baby."

"That was a different time, and it wasn't my choice."

"Are you saying you didn't want to do it?" I asked.

"I am stating that no one asked me. "I wanted to sing," Mom explained. "I worked hard at it. I had a recording contract. But then I became pregnant and had you to care for, and that is the life I chose." She said it as if she had just turned the page from one chapter to the next. I couldn't read the expression on her face.

If you ask my mother how she handles difficult conversations, she responds, "I go like this." She draws her hand down across her face like a curtain, and when she folds her hands back into her lap, she has the flawless smile of a Stepford wife. So perfect. So beautiful. It's a skill I eventually acquired. My stepford smile. It gets a lot of play.

We didn't necessarily have Mom and Dad's approval, but we began booking jobs. We felt we could go out, perform the job, and return home without Mom and Dad knowing. Most of the time, it worked, but every now and then, someone would call our mother and say, "Oh, yeah, I just saw Paris and Nicky shooting over at [whatever place]," and then we had to face her when we were home. She disliked it, but we worked on her willpower.

Three Possible Reasons Mom Did Not Want Us to Work as Models

She knew more about modeling and acting than we did, and she didn't want us to have to learn the hard way.

It was difficult for her to see us working since it triggered a lot of "what ifs" in her head. Seeing Nicky with her lovely children triggers "what ifs" in my mind.

In February 1997, I turned sixteen. I wanted my party to be in LA so that Gram Cracker, Papa, Nanu, and all of my LA cousins and friends could attend. Mom collaborated with Brent Bolthouse and Jen Rosero to plan an unforgettable sweet-sixteen party at Pop, a

Highland club for kids under the age of eighteen on Thursdays and Saturdays. That was one of my first nights out in Hollywood, and it was without a doubt the loveliest sweet sixteen I'd ever attended.

My mother threw an incredible party.

Everybody was dressed to kill. Brent brought in DJ AM. Nicky, I, and all of our buddies felt very mature. We are at this club! With this incredible DJ! And we look stunning! It was thrilling.

"You were bright-eyed and bushy-tailed," Brent says now in a big-brotherly tone, although I didn't feel like a child anymore. Before I went out onto any runway, I looked in the mirror and saw a woman staring back at me. It helped that Wonderbra was popular—perhaps because the fashion was for women to be slender, resulting in a naturally flat chest. Wonderbra debuted in the 1960s, during the reign of the bullet bra, and was poised for a comeback. I embraced that dynamic and made it work for me, and subsequently, around 2015, I created my own fantasy push-up bras under the Paris Hilton brand.

I have to be careful about wearing push-up bras these days because they always ignite rumors that I'm pregnant, and the most frustrating thing that could possibly happen when you want to have a baby is continual Twitter and tabloid speculations that make people say, "Paris looks pregnant. Paris, are you pregnant? Still not pregnant? How about now? You appear pregnant. "Why are you not pregnant?" Ugh. Stop chatting. It is beyond.

Wait. What did we talk about? Reverse engineer for a second.

Wonderbra.

Bolthouse.

Sweet sixteen.

Yaasssss! I felt ready to take on the world. I was excited to drive. You can travel anywhere in New York by cab or metro, but I believed I'd spend most of my time in Los Angeles if I pursued modeling, acting, and music, which appeared to be my path. Veterinary school was not for me, but I liked the notion of utilizing my position to advocate for animals, as Tippi Hedren and Brigitte Bardot had done.

Because I wasn't in school, I could sleep in and feel well rested when I went out at night to see the city. There was always something intriguing going on, beautiful clothes to admire, fascinating people to observe, and dancing to do. The challenge of slipping out felt like a game, and I was adept at it. When 30H was dark and quiet, I'd tiptoe down the hall in my tracksuit and sneakers. I pulled my pals along with me if they were willing, and I met a lot of new people who were night owls like myself.

Mom and Dad were killing it—running numerous business ventures and managing enormous teams—which should have made it easy for me to come and go whenever I wanted, but Mom's a clever cookie. If she came across a business card or cocktail napkin with a phone number on it, she transformed the 1 to a 7 or the 3 to an 8. I'd phone these folks, and they'd say, "What the hell?"

Nicky was a constant complainer. Except when she wanted to go out with me. But this was only on weekends. She stayed at home most school nights. Not me.

When the school year finished, we headed to the Hamptons, where everyone was calmer and happier, in beach mode, until we learned that Princess Diana had been killed in a wild car chase while evading the media. Nicky and I were distraught. We adored Princess Diana. Now she was in Heaven with Marilyn, forever youthful and perfect. We didn't consider why everyone wants women to stay youthful if death is the only option to do so. And I didn't relate her death to the paparazzi that waited for me outside the clubs at night. To me, they were just a group of well-meaning, ordinary sweeties. So flattering and humorous.

We were on the other side of the looking glass at the time, eating all of the tabloid photos that made Diana an icon.

"They killed her," Mom stated plainly. "They hunted her down like a pack of coyotes." Do you see now? Do you understand what I've been telling you?"

I did, but in order to flourish as a model, I needed to be noticed. I needed to be out there getting photographed.

We returned to New York, and, as my parents had anticipated, images of me began to appear in the tabloids. Dad was silently furious. Mom sobbed every day. They were enraged that I was breaking their hearts, being a poor influence on my siblings, wasting my life, and acting like a pampered, out-of-control brat. It was the same conversation over and over.

THEM: "What are people thinking right now—that we let our kids run around town all night?" What should we do? "Move to the Moon?"

ME: "Oh my God! Leave me alone! "I'm so sick of this conversation."

It was horrible.

Mom practically locked me in my room at night, but I was resourceful and managed to escape a few times a week. I could sometimes persuade Barron by promising him that if he stole the key from Mom's room, he could accompany me. Whispering through the locked door, I prepared him with tales of the wonderland that is New York at night, telling him how we would dance, consume candy, and eat as much McDonald's as we wanted. He'd go fetch that key, trusting me completely.

"Okay, now go to bed and sleep," I instructed him. "I'll come and get you when it's time to go out."

What—that did not happen! I lied. Please. He was in second grade. Even though I had some standards.

Sometimes party nights lasted days, and when I got home, Mom was sitting on my bed, crying. Gram Cracker arrived and stayed for a week, and I hoped she'd be on my side, but she wasn't. She slept on a cot outside my bedroom door, so I could not open it without her knowledge.

I knew I was scaring my folks.

I knew it was cruel. And risky.

I adored my family and resented myself for causing them pain.

I truly don't understand some of my decisions, and I would never encourage any fifteen-year-old to drop out of school and party for 36 hours a day.

ADHD, whether diagnosed or undiagnosed, does not give you permission to sabotage your family or put yourself at risk. I am not using my ADHD as an excuse. But I'm wondering. What if the therapist I visited back then, who I dismissed as a joke, had diagnosed and treated my ADHD? What if someone at any of the schools I attended sought to help rather than repair me? I wonder how things would have been different if my parents had said, "We don't like modeling, but we'll help you if you agree to a few ground rules." I wish they had said that. Maybe they said it, but I don't remember. Trauma frequently strips a person of their surrounding memories, which is uncomfortable but merciful.

I'm really trying to figure out what this circumstance was like for my parents. Because I will never comprehend what they choose to do about it.

"To save your baby—you'd do it, too," Mom adds on rare occasions when she's willing to discuss it. She says that with perfect surety, even now that she understands how everything went wrong. "You would do the same."

Not in a million fucking years, I believe, but I don't say it out loud. I can't bring myself to disagree with her because I can't face the notion of ever being separated from my family again. Instead, I wrap my arms around her neck and say the one true thing I can say: "I love you, Mom."

South Park had its Comedy Central debut in the autumn of 1997.

The first Harry Potter book is published.

Madeleine Albright became the first female Secretary of State.

Bell bottoms and platform shoes came out of the closet, teamed with cropped tanks and anything with a Union Jack to celebrate the Spice Girls' Cool Britannia movement.

"I knew there was a takedown in the works," Nicky explained later, "but I didn't know the details."

My final night at home was unremarkable. I ate dinner with my family. Mom cooked. We ate. We chatted and joked. Nobody appeared furious, weird, or nervous. I chose to remain in that night. I'm not sure if that decision aided or hurt the "takedown" plan.

I talked on the phone with pals before going to bed. I was dead sleeping when my bedroom door broke open around 4:30 a.m., and someone ripped the covers off of me. A large hand grabbed my ankle and dragged me off the mattress. I was immediately awake—hyper awake—in a state of fear, yelling and struggling. My mind immediately turned to the obvious.

I'm about to get raped. I am about to be murdered.

This is where the recollection shatters—a broken mirror in my head.

Two dudes.

Hands on me.

Coffee breath.

Body odor.

One of them placed a sweaty palm over my mouth, forcing my head back and cutting off the breath I needed to scream. The other held up a set of handcuffs that mirrored the light in the hallway. The way he dangled them in his dirty fingers suggested he was having fun.

He responded: "Do you want to go the easy way or the hard way?"

I went the hard way.

I attempted to break free by clawing, kicking, and yelling. One man held my upper torso, while the other held my legs. My thrashing only strengthened their grip as they hauled me out into the corridor.

This is a nightmare. This is a nightmare.

I kept trying to rouse myself up, as I do now. For decades, I replayed the scene in my imagination every night.

I notice this girl wearing a flimsy Hello Kitty nightshirt. She spins in panic and screams, "Mom! Dad! "Help me!"

And then I see my mother and father.

Their bedroom door is broken open just enough for them to peer over the edge, their cheeks smeared with weeping. They squeeze against each other, watching as two strangers pull me out the door and into the darkness.

CHAPTER 5

TOUGH LOVE

The back of the black SUV was ingeniously rigged so that the doors and windows couldn't be opened from the inside. The two men were like big, 'roided-up meatheads, so they had no problem putting me in there, even though I was kicking and struggling with every ounce of strength I had. As the Waldorf vanished behind me, I collapsed into a ball, seized by a strange, uncontrollable trembling. I was trembling so hard that I thought my teeth were going to rattle out of my mouth. Looking back, I realize I was in shock. I must have been crying because they kept telling me to stop talking.

At first, I figured my mother was correct: someone had seen me in the tabloids and was kidnapping me for ransom, so I begged and pleaded with them, "Please, whatever you want—my parents will pay you."

They laughed. One of them said, "You brought this upon yourself. Your parents had no choice. "They are doing this for your own good."

My parents—what now?

"You're gonna learn," one kidnapper stated. "You're gonna get schooled."

"What the fuck, what the fuck?"

(Typically, the therapist recommends the transportation service. They claim it's easier for everyone. Definitely worth a few thousand dollars.

On the drive to the airport, they explained that my parents had hired them to take me to a "special boarding school" in California. They offered proof: my mother had packed a small bag for me including socks, underwear, toiletries, family photos, and a basic wardrobe of casual school clothes. They informed me that the place they were sending me was hidden high in the mountains, and that the counselors there would employ "tough love" to correct my problems.

"There's nothing wrong with me," I said. "I am not going there. I'm not boarding any fucking plane with you."

The kidnapper flashed me the handcuffs again. "Up to you. Do you want to board the plane quietly, or do you want to be handcuffed?"

"Fuck you!" I kicked the back of the seat, and they laughed.

"Do that again, and I'll have to restrain you," he responded. "For your own safety, of course."

At the airport, they gave me a velour tracksuit and sneakers from Mom's packed luggage. I climbed into my soft, familiar garments, relieved for the final semblance of home. This was before 9/11, so coming into the airport and boarding a flight was a very different experience. You just entered and headed to the gate. Walking through the terminal, I kept my eyes down, as if everyone was watching me. I wasn't quite famous back then, but in New York, I was frequently recognized—that Hilton girl, that socialite wild child from Page Six—so I didn't want to stroll through JFK in handcuffs.

"I'll be fine," I promised myself in my baby voice, determined to be calm and rational. Flanking me and grasping my arms, these two refrigerator-sized men guided me down the concourse, and I ran between them, looking for any conceivable way out.

There were none. This was happening.

They were pros, trained to cover all bases. I had no choice but to go along with it till I figured out how to get away. Crammed into the middle seat between them, I attempted to sound thrilled to start my new school. Oh, what? Is it in the mountains? How cool is that? I smiled and feigned to sleep, thinking they could drag me to this boarding school but not force me to stay. I was confident. I had plenty of practice sneaking out of the house and avoiding guys who came too close on the dance floor. As soon as the sun set, I'd leave.

My confidence plummeted as we traveled eighty miles from LAX to Running Springs, California. The route snaked up into the San Bernardino Mountains. Cars became farther apart and more run down. Trees grew taller and closer together. My ears throbbed with the increasing altitude. My eyes stung from fatigue. A cold, tight knot formed in my gut.

We approached an iron gate. It opened.

We drove in. It clanged shut.

The Walter Huston Lodge was created by Anjelica Huston's Academy Award-winning grandfather in the 1930s. He was an engineer first and an actor second. The huge, ancient structure had a massive stone fireplace, towering ceilings, and thirteen guest rooms for his Hollywood friends. It was a fantastic spot to escape from it all. Away from inquisitive eyes.

Huston died in 1950, and I believe the building lay empty until CEDU bought it in 1967. The school had been evicted from its prior location by neighbors who maintained that the zoning, which allowed for a school, did not allow for CEDU because this location—no matter how Wasserman attempted to market it—was not a school. Freaky stories and scary rumors circulated. Weird things happened there. Sex orgies, drugs, chanting and yelling. There's so much yelling. They did not want it in their neighborhood, so CEDU moved to Huston's secluded mountain retreat.

A good spot to escape from it all.

I was taken into the lodge. I remember a room with two employees: a messy-looking hippie guy and a disgusting woman with a pointed weasel face.

(No offense to weasels. (Love you.)

Four or five other students, both male and female, stood observing. Weaselmug closed the door and announced, "I need to search you for contraband. "Take off your clothing."

I replied, "No, that's not it—I swear I don't have anything. How would I get anything? I was at home. "I was asleep."

"Take off your jacket."

When I refused to take it off, she reiterated the line about "the easy way or the hard way," claiming it was pointless to resist what was about to happen because my parents had given them medical power of attorney and she could inject me with sedatives if she chose.

I unzipped the jacket and gave it to her.

The next several minutes are mostly white noise in my thoughts, but I can still hear her voice, flat and monotonous, like a broken shutter slamming in the wind.

Take off your shoes.

Take off your sock.

Take off your shirts.

Take off your bra.

Take off your pants.

Take off your underwear.

She delivered each garment to someone, who ran his hands over every seam before stuffing it into a bag. I vaguely recall standing naked in front of all those people, shaking uncontrollably, my knees locked together, my arms wrapped tightly about my chest.

When she started cavity searching, I assumed it was a dental examination. That's the only time I'd ever heard the phrase cavity.

Weaselmug saw that I didn't understand and stated, "We have to make sure you don't have drugs or weapons hidden in there."

"In . . . where?"

I couldn't understand what she was saying. Because she was unable to verbalize what she was saying. That couldn't happen. Everyone else stood there, with expressions like—I'm not sure.

I do not know.

Just... terrible.

Staring at me. Snickering. They shuffled their feet. These boys were not much older than myself.

The woman put on a latex glove and asked, "Are you going to cooperate, or do we need to have these guys hold you down and pull your legs apart?"

I despised the whining rabbit sound that came out of me. It wasn't my smart baby voice; it was real panic.

"Let's go," she replied. "Squat down and cough."

I squatted and tried to cough, but all I could manage was sobbing and gasping for air.

"Are you going to cooperate, or—"

I had a hard cough.

She felt around between my legs and then forced me to stand up, lean forward, and keep my butt cheeks apart as she probed inside me with her gloved fingers. When it was over, she gave me some stained magenta sweatpants. They were disgusting, but whatever. I was desperate to cover myself. I put on the sweatpants without protest and wiped my nose with the sleeve.

"We're gonna keep her in pink," Weaselmug stated. "Transport says she's probably a runner."

She handed me socks. No shoes.

"Shoes are a privilege you'll have to earn."

I understand she intended to humiliate me with those terrible magenta sweatpants, but pink has always been my power color. My walking style is unaffected by what I'm wearing. Do you think a model likes every look that is imposed on her? At sixteen, I had worn some beautiful costumes on the runway, but I'd also worn some horror outfits. I'd previously learnt that the walk starts from within. You wear the clothes; they do not wear you.

On the set of Paris in Love in 2021, I was filming a funny little dream scenario in which I zoomed down the street to a chapel on a Razor scooter, dressed in a bridal mini with pink living gloves, angel wings, and platform heels so high that the producer was concerned.

"Paris," she asked. "How do you feel about riding a scooter in those heels? Do you feel confident about that?"

"I'll do anything in heels," I replied.

"I love that answer, but . . ."

"I was born in heels."

She scrawled something on her clipboard and stated, "I'm literally saying that. "Just so you know."

I changed it to "I was born in Louboutins" and was about to post it on Instagram when I received a FaceTime call from Rebecca Mellinger, head of impact at 11:11 Media and now 11:11 Impact, the foundation I founded to channel all of my frustration and sadness about the troubled-teen industry into meaningful action. Nowadays, impact is an important aspect of my company model. It does not generate revenue, yet it is the most important aspect. It benefits people, which makes it quite fulfilling.

Rebecca is a determined administrative warrior who leads my legislative efforts, manages media relations, and plans events. We were in the midst of obtaining congressional support for a bill of rights mandating openness and other safeguards in congregate-care facilities. I was stepping into the conversation as needed, despite the fact that I was in the midst of wedding preparations and a hectic shooting schedule.

"Senator Merkley has a couple of questions," Rebecca remarked. She handed the phone over to Senator Jeff Merkley of Oregon, who, along with Representatives Ro Khanna (CA-17), Buddy Carter (GA-01), Rosa DeLauro (CT-03), Adam Schiff (CA-28), and Senator John Cornyn of Texas, supported this measure.

I held the phone at arm's length, just over my right temple. (Another essential right: your ideal photo viewpoint.) I didn't feel the need to explain the glittery angel wings because whatever you're wearing is a reflection of your location, not your identity. You rock it and accomplish your tasks.

"Senator Merkley," I continued, "I appreciate your support. We need to improve the private referrals aspect of this. As stated, the emphasis is on children who pass through the foster-care and juvenile-justice systems."

I straightened my shoulders and flexed my angel wings.

"I appreciate the need to advocate for children in foster care," I replied, "but I can tell you from personal experience that many of these kids come from wonderful parents. Wealthy dwellings. Their parents are duped and screwed over. Transparency is their only hope. "I will not abandon those kids."

Rebecca ended the call, and I sped out to church on my scooter.

I can accomplish anything in heels.

CHAPTER 6

LOCKED AWAY

A girl with a bland expression and mousy hair led me to a room with four bunk beds. I can't recall her name, so I'll simply call her Blanda.

"This is you," Blanda replied brightly, pointing to the top bunk with a yellow cushion and blanket. "I am over on that side. There are sometimes four people in here, but right now it's just us. "I'm your big sister."

"No," I replied. "You aren't. I have a sister. "It is not you."

I crawled up onto the bunk and curled into a ball, thinking the ceiling would collapse on this woman.

"Yeah," she answered. "I read in your profile that you have a younger sister. Little brothers. I am an only child. "But now I have you, little sister!"

"Please stop talking."

"This is for your own benefit. I saw in your profile that you were expelled out of every school in the world for using drugs and sleeping around.

"That's bullshit," I said. "That's not true."

"Now is not the moment to vent your rage, Paris. Wait for Rap tonight, and then care for your emotions."

I buried my head with my arms, wondering what that meant.

"I need to talk to my mom," I said. "I need to call my mom right now."

"Perhaps in a few weeks. "That's a privilege you'll have to earn," Blanda explained. She gave me a big binder. "Here's everything about what to do and what not do, a glossary of terms you need to memorize, and all the stuff you'll need to work on in each of the Prophets."

"Whatever."

"You cannot stay up there. I'm expected to show you around and familiarize you with the regulations.

"Don't bother," I replied. "I'm not staying."

"Don't say that!" Blanda muttered, wide-eyed and urgent. "You will get us both into trouble. If you try to flee, they will apprehend you and make you regret it. If you don't follow the program and stick to the agreement, you'll wind up at Ascent. Or even Provo. Trust me, you don't want to be sent to Provo. We only want to help you, Paris. We simply want you to understand yourself and nurture the child within you, your tiny you. You'll be shocked at how quickly the next two years go by."

"Two years?" I got down from the bunk to look into her face and check whether she was fucking with me. "Two years?"

"You'll graduate when you're eighteen, and you won't want to leave. Many of the team leaders and counselors are grads. They are obligated to work on the program alongside us."

"How long have you been here?" I asked.

"Two years and a bit. It went like that." She snaps her fingers. "I wish it was longer. I'm dreading turning 18. C'mon. There is a lot of stuff to cover. Begin with the basics: this is your drawer."

She pulled open a wooden drawer. It had underwear and socks, but they belonged to someone else.

"Before breakfast, they inspect the drawers, mattresses, floor, and the entire room. If you do not follow the rules, you will be written up or banned. Bans are when you can't talk to anyone and no one can talk to you. For example, if you're on a male ban, you can't look at or talk to boys, and they can't look at or talk to you.

I walked over the mountainside in my socks, attempting to step over slushy places and autumn snowdrifts. I witnessed children moving boulders, excavating trenches, and stacking cinder blocks to form a retaining wall. There was a tennis court with no net, a horse stable with no horses, and a storage room with cleaning supplies packed on shelves. Blanda showed me the kitchen, where children were opening cans, and the laundry room, where someone else was folding towels. She showed me a cement shower room with multiple shower heads on the wall and drains on the floor, but no separators or curtains. Scrubbing was done by two girls on their hands and knees.

"Don't look at them," Blanda whispered. "They're on bans."

All the time, she chartered away, reciting a long list of strange rules.

There is no swearing, singing, humming, or throat clearing.

No dancing, skipping, or spinning.

No touching, hugging, kissing, or holding hands.

Avoid crossing your legs. No shuffling your feet.

No whistling.

No noisy breathing or lip-smacking while eating.

No chatting about music, sports, television shows, movies, news events, your parents, siblings, friends, your clothes, your room, your school, or anything else related to your home.

No mention of Marilyn Manson.

There is no mention of candy, pizza, hot dogs, cheeseburgers, lasagna, McDonald's, Burger King, or Wendy's.

We're not talking about bicycles, skateboards, or inline skates.

No peeking out the window without permission. No opening a door without authorization. No going to the restroom without authorization. No asking for permission to use the restroom, open a door, or gaze out a window.

Please do not request food or water. No eating outside of mealtime. No uneaten food on your plate. There is no asking why or why not.

No eye rolling.

No sighing.

No snoring.

No slouching.

No shrugging.

No fidgeting, nail biting, skin picking, or scratching.

No whining. No crying. No yelling.

"Except during Rap," she explained. "During Raps, you must participate. Really get in there and utilize your loud voice. If you do not participate, you will be astounded. If you find someone who isn't following the program or keeping in agreement, you should definitely call them out during Rap. Report them to a counselor. If you don't report, you're just as guilty as the rule-breaker, right? And if you don't tell them, you're actually injuring them by preventing them from performing their emotional work."

I was beginning to appreciate the need for a glossary. Bans, raps, prophets, agreement/disagreement, doing the program, managing your anger, and caring for your feelings—it was a lot. There is also a lot of crap. The rulebook was a maze of arrangements, making it impossible to avoid penalties. As if the entire thing was engineered to make you suffer and fail.

That night, in those awful pink sweatpants on the higher bunk, I sobbed for hours. I eventually fell into a headachy half-sleep, but I kept waking up from a nightmare—a hand grasping my ankle, a grubby palm clamped over my mouth—and then I sobbed until I dozed again, repeating the cycle until Blanda poked me and whispered, "Paris. It's five thirty. "We have to clean the room."

We made the beds, organized our drawers, and cleaned every surface, including the floor. There was no mirror, but I caught a glimpse of my face through the glass, and I looked exhausted.

"You're not allowed to look out the window!" Blanda hissed, and I wondered why there weren't any curtains if they didn't want you to see out the window? Before I turned away, I tried to catch a breath of sunlight.

Someone arrived to inspect the room and allowed us to eat breakfast, which consisted of some grayish hot cereal. Jobs were assigned. I dimly recall a bunch of girls and a few guys hauling wood from a stack at the bottom of a hill to another stack halfway up. Eventually, we were directed to a table for lunch. Two slices of bread and one slice of bologna. After lunch, we worked for a few more hours when Weaselmug screamed that it was time to shower.

We proceeded to the showers, and the females began to undress. I just stood there. A half-dozen staff members, both male and female, stood against the wall, watching the teenage females undress and shower. These guys and women interacted, joked, and made pervy remarks.

I stood at the doorway.

Like, frozen.

Like, what the actual fuck.

The naked girls' lifeless looks as they bathed themselves with lukewarm spray were the most unsettling. They were used to it. This was their lives. They simply accepted it.

Weaselmug slammed her knuckles into the back of my skull, asking, "What are you waiting for, an invitation?"

A middle-aged male guard asked, "Need help with your panties?" and the rest of them laughed.

Staring at the floor and attempting to face the wall, I stripped and bathed as quickly as I could while the staff made cow and dog noises and lame jokes about carpet not matching curtains. I wrapped a scratchy towel over myself and shivered until we were allowed to return to our rooms.

Whoever was doing the wash had left clean socks and pink sweatpants on my bed.

"When do I get my own clothes back?" I inquired of Blanda.

"After they're labeled, I suppose. "But you won't need those," she explained. "They'll give you whatever they want you to wear."

I had only slept a few hours in the previous three days, so I stated I wanted to lie down and forgo dinner.

"Dinner's not optional," Blanda said. "And after dinner, we go to Rap."

I don't recall what we ate for dinner, but I forced myself to swallow every last bite after a girl across from me muttered, "If you don't eat it, they'll feed it to you."

We went to the "Rap" thing when we were quite little, probably about five or six. I can't separate that night from any other because this strange thing happened multiple times a week for three or four hours. I'll try to express it, but I'm not sure whether you'll really comprehend it unless you're experiencing it.

A group of people sat in a circle of chairs.

Loud music was played through the house speakers.

I don't mean loud music; I mean music that is played loudly.

It was always some stupid soft rock or easy-listening song—John Denver or Kenny Rogers or something—and I don't recall ever hearing a woman's voice. I'm trying to think of some specifics, but I've mostly shut those songs out. Fellow survivors have cited Randy VanWarmer's song "Just When I Needed You Most," and I recall it being played a lot at CEDU and the CEDU sister schools where I was later kept. You've undoubtedly heard that in the elevator. The chorus says, "Youuuuuuuuuuuuuuuu left me just when I needed you the most."

This one song played on repeat while everyone sat down, and the team leaders—Weaselmug, Hippie Mess, and recent graduates who now work here on some sort of fucked-up Stockholm Syndrome career path—went around and spooled off paper towels in little piles here and there, then strategically placed the rolls around the circle.

"What the hell..." I murmured.

The guy next to me puffed and half-laughed, saying, "Whatever you think you know—you don't."

Around the circle, children withdrew within themselves, resembling hamsters in a snake pit. Or they sat on the edge of their seats, eyes wide, waiting for the game to start.

"Blanda, would you like to start?" Weaselmug said.

Blanda stood in front of the boy next to me and said, "Jason, I just saw you talking to Paris." Aren't you on a girl ban because you winked at Deirdre last week? I mean, it's out of agreement, and you probably think you're going to fuck one or both of them, which is a complete fantasy, because no self-respecting girl would fuck a fat, ugly slob like you. It will never happen, but you are so oblivious that you don't even realize what a terrible human being you are. I know you are secretly gay. I saw in your file about your child molester uncle, and it appears that he doesn't even want you around anymore. "What does that tell you?"

I was waiting for this dude to tell her to quiet up or go screw herself. He sat there, staring at the floor and saying nothing.

"Where's that selfish desire coming from, Jason?" Hippie Mess inquired. "Was that I or Me staring at Paris and Deirdre with selfish, filthy thoughts and vile sexual fantasies? Was I the liar, or was I the feeler?"

"I," the fellow muttered.

"Right! Look! Weaselmug said, "Look at what you're doing right now." "I am biting Man's lip!"

"Selfish asshole," exclaimed another girl. "We're always on bans. Too stupid to use the program. Too selfish, foolish, and lazy to perform emotional labor. It's no surprise his family was saying, "Get the fuck out, you piece of crap." Because nobody can stand you. Not even those who are legally obligated.

Like a floodgate opening, people piled on, everyone talking at once, their voices entwined in that strange, loud sound. What a jerk off! Why are you still alive, you piece of garbage? Your family can't handle the fact that you left me since you're terrible at everything.

You pretend you're a writer—as if you're going to publish a book someday and rat everyone out. In the meantime, you're too stupid to spell your own name, you useless piece of shit. Why don't you YOUUUUUUUUUU LEFT ME kill yourself and put everyone out of their misery? Oh, I forgot—you tried and couldn't even do it correctly.

This continued on and on and on for what seemed like an eternity until his face crumpled and tears ran from his eyes, and they kept at it and at it and at it and at it until he bent forward with his face in his hands, screaming like an injured animal.

"Run your anger, Jason," Hippie Mess urged. "Take care of your feelings."

The male sobbed deeply, ripping sobs, choking on the words, "I can't—I can't—I'm a piece of shit, and I try—and—and I tried not to look at her, and I was thinking about wanting to—to see her—and like—wanting to jerk off because I'm a sick piece of shit! "I am weak, perverted, and a dumb-shit asshole!"

Tears and slimy boogers dropped over the floor in front of him. Weaselmug pushed a wad of paper towels over with her foot.

"I want to know why Paris hasn't said anything," one of the girls remarked. "She's just sitting there like a prissy little stuck-up rich bitch."

"Uh, you don't know me," I responded; "and what happened to the no-swearing rule?"

Hippie Mess winked at me and said, "Talk dirty, but live clean."

"You were right to put her in pinks," Blanda replied. "She told me she was going to run." "She said the program is bullshit, all the girls here are fat, stupid pigs, and if she can't get out, she'll burn this place down."

I clinched my teeth and exclaimed, "Fuck you, Blanda." I've never said that.``

"I heard you were slacking on chores," Weaselmug explained.

She was slacking! She was slacking." Jason hiccuped. "She was mincing around like she was too good for everybody while I went up the fucking hill eight hundred times."

"I don't have any shoes, you moron."

As soon as I said it, I realized it was a mistake to defend myself. The entire circle zeroed in on me, a creature with saucer eyes and black hole jaws.

"You'll get used to it," Blanda said softly.

No, I promised myself. I will not.

CHAPTER 7

ESCAPE

My recall of the weeks that followed is a fog of shock and tiredness. I stumbled through each day in my pink sweatpants and gym socks, attempting to avoid speaking or being spoken to, swallowing my shame and dread, and avoiding eye contact with the lads who hissed and spit at me during Rap. If they looked at me, they would see that I was the one who got into trouble.

I counted down the fourteen days until I could call my folks and wear shoes again.

"Two weeks," I told Hippie Mess in my finest baby voice. "You told me I could call my parents. "I can't wait to tell them how lovely it is here."

He smiled and remarked, "That's cool." Blanda and I will be right next to you. To assist you."

Oh.

My parents had been warned by the psychiatrist, who paid weekly visits to the school, that I would lie and manipulate them into allowing me to come home. He advised them that the only way to literally save my life was to stand firm and refuse to listen to my begging and pleading.

When I sat down for my fifteen-minute phone call, Hippie Mess and Blanda sat right beside me, listening in. I had meant to say everything as quickly as possible before they cut me off, but when I heard my mother's voice, my throat choked up and I began crying.

"Mom . ..Mom . .."

I needed those fucking sneakers. I was hesitant to say anything that might give the counselors a reason to keep me in pink, so I tried to send Mom a covert message. I utilized the baby voice, which she recognized as false AF. (Who do you think I learned that from?)

"Mom, I just. ..It's like. ..I am very. ..Yes, truly. ." I could not do it. Words flowed out of my lips. "Mom, please!" You need to get me out of here! This place is fucked up! You don't know!"

"Paris, honey, I understand how hard it is. You just have to persevere and stick with the regimen."

Work the program?

My mother's use of CEDU-speak scared me. I'd assumed my folks had no idea what was going on. Now I wasn't sure what to think.

"Mom, they—this isn't like—like, in the shower—"

Hippie Mess gently but firmly snatched the phone from me, saying, "That's all for today, Paris."

I tried to cling onto the receiver. "No! No, I have fifteen minutes!"

"Paris," he replied, "you don't want to lose your calling privileges, do you?""

"I will not say anything nasty. I will not tell. "I swear.

He hung up the phone, cutting off the connection—that tiny thread of affection in my mother's voice. It would have been less painful if he had severed my finger.

"Do you want to make another call two weeks from now?"

"Yes."

"Okay, then. "Work the program."

Another week passed by. And then another.

I felt so fatigued. I tried everything to fall asleep—counting, playing music in my head, envisioning myself dancing beneath the strobe lights—but the second the blanket touched my foot, I startled wide awake, my pulse pounding out of my chest because I was back in that moment with the thug clutching my ankle.

I jumped out of bed in the morning and cleaned the room. If there was a hair on a pillowcase or a wrinkle in the blanket, the team leader would dismantle my bunk, empty my drawer, and instruct me to start again. And then they'd rip apart Blanda's belongings to make her detest me. They didn't always give us a reason; sometimes they just trashed the room to annoy us and make us miss breakfast.

Working outside in stocking feet was uncomfortable, but working inside was far worse. Working inside entailed scrubbing toilets and floors while creepy staff members hung around smoking, leering, and making frightening remarks to girls who were down on their hands and knees. Outside, there was chilly, pure air, and carrying rocks and logs to the top of the hill provided a greater perspective of the surroundings. It appeared to be miles and miles of nothing but trees, but every now and then, I noticed dust rising from a gravel road or a puff of smoke from a chimney, giving me an idea of where the town may be.

I forced myself to eat foods that I wouldn't feed a dog in order to stay strong. I lifted my head and drank shower spray to replace the insufficient water we were provided after hours of physical labor.

Stay hydrated. Stay beautiful. Be prepared to climb out a window.

During "school" hours, we were expected to create "dirt lists" and "disclosures," admitting to all of our "cop-outs"—sins, evil ideas, and horrible things we had done or had been done to us. These confessions were used as ammo for Rap. I refused to jump in there and blow people away, so I was continuously banned, but I never offered anything substantial on my dirt list, so they could only blow me away with the scant material in my file.

These shattered CEDU individuals studied cruelty as if it were a martial art: mostly for self-defense but lethal when necessary. The person being blown away would sit there with large, wounded, tearful eyes, and it was tempting to pounce at that moment. You need to feel protected, yet being a bully involves a fragile shell of authority. However, that layer of safety is fragile and unstable, and what goes around comes around, so the bullies were more afraid than everyone else. The children who caused the harm were as damaged as the children they abused.

The nightly smoosh was simply—ugh. Beyond. There was no escaping it. Thinking about that makes me want to soak in a tub of sea salt and hand sanitizer. We all did what we needed to do to survive, and it left lasting wounds. I'm not sure who those kids were or whether they'll ever see this, but it wasn't their fault. Or mine. None of it. The cinder block of shame we carried out of that place was never ours to bear. It belongs to the people who created that location.

After about a month, I was told I was going to my first Prophet. Each Propheet has a theme, such as the "I & Me Propheet," the "Journey of Self Propheet," or the "Whatever-the-fuck-ever Propheet"—it didn't matter to me. You had to sit through several hours of lectures by team leaders and counselors who read from lengthy scripts produced by the great god of furniture sales, Wasserman himself.

There were strange exercises, such as one in which a child had to lie on the floor, a "trainer" placed a towel into their mouth, and the child had to bite down and try to keep their head on the floor as the "trainer" yanked on the towel, attempting to lift them. (And, yes, this is as violent as it sounds; there were reports of individuals losing teeth and a girl whose jaw was so screwed up that she had surgery.)

Following that, there was a marathon mega-Rap that began in the evening and continued till the morning. You had to stay up and involved in this routine until breakfast the next day—and that was the first food or water you received during the entire bizarre event.

This was a large group event that largely took place outside and involved a lot of physical activity, so thank you, God! They handed me shoes. I made sure I sat near the perimeter. Two or three hours into the lesson, when everyone was expected to stand up and chant, I approached the adjacent enforcers and said, "Hello, boys!" in a pleasant, flirtatious manner that the paparazzi always enjoyed.

One of them said, "Hi."

The other one said, "Get back in your group, Hilton."

"I really, really need to visit the little girls' room," I added, laughing. "Only a short tinkling. Pleeeeease?"

The first enforcer grinned and looked to the front of the group. Everyone was raising their hands in the air, making it impossible for the speaker to see us. The enforcer motioned to the restrooms and urged, "Hurry."

I'd scrub toilets there numerous times while mentally measuring the window. It was small and high on the wall, but I was tall and extremely thin from a month of hard work and poor diet. I climbed onto the toilet, clawed my way over the ledge, and fell to the ground on the opposite side of the building. I darted across the yard, stayed in the darkness, climbed the fence, and ran like hell. Without turning back, I scrambled down a steep embankment, through dense underbrush, and into the mossy woodland.

People were always saying, "Don't go into the forest." There are dead kids in there. "If you try to flee, they will kill you and hide your body in the woods."

I didn't believe that, and it wouldn't have made a difference. All that mattered was getting out of there. I don't remember thinking anything other than "run, run." I headed downhill instinctively. I noticed a gravel path beneath me and followed it until I reached a small brook. I didn't want my shoes to get wet, so I crossed the road and curved down the mountain until I reached a paved road.

Every time I heard a car approaching, I jumped the guardrail and hid in a ditch or behind bushes.

It was late afternoon. The sun went below the ridge. I was chilly and afraid, yet I was bursting with adrenaline. I felt as if I were in a movie. This was some James Bond crap! I ran for what seemed like a long time, staying close to the road and avoiding incoming automobiles. I'm not sure how far. Eventually, I noticed a bright yard light through the trees and followed it to a small parking lot outside a roadside travel stop that resembled a combination restaurant and gas station. There was a pay phone on the side of the building.

Oh, God. Thank you.

Remember pay phones? Do pay phones still exist? Thinking about how pleased and relieved I was to see the dirty outdoor phone nailed to a pole makes me want to buy one and put it in my doorway.

Using a method that all club kids know, I lifted the receiver and toggled the flippy device underneath until an operator appeared.

"Operator," she said. "Do you require assistance?""

"Yes! I need to place a collect call to—" Fuck. I wasn't sure who to call. My parents might not listen. Gram Cracker was too far away to do anything. "I need to call Kyle Richards."

I gave her my aunt's telephone number.

The operator inquired, "Who should I say is calling?""

"Star," I answered.

Kyle responded and acknowledged the charges. "Paris, honey—"

"Kyle, you need to save me. Please. And do not tell Mom. Please come and grab me, Kyle. Please. Please hurry. This place is fucked up. People are quite abusive, and Mom doesn't—"

"What exactly do you mean by abusive?" Did any of the other kids hit you?"

"No, it is not—please." I'll let you know when you get here. You need to come right now. Please. "I need you to get me out of here."

"Where are you?""She inquired, and I gave her the address written on a card next to a taxi ad.

"Okay, just wait there," Kyle replied. "Don't go anywhere."

I went behind the building and crouched in the weeds. After a while, a police cruiser pulled into the parking lot.

"Have you seen any blond girls?" the cop inquired as someone exited the establishment.

Shit. Shit. Think. Think. Think. Hide.

A door in the back of the run-down building was stuck open, most likely venting heat from the kitchen, and there was a narrow stairwell just inside. As soon as the cop left, I sneaked up the stairs and walked behind some boxes of Christmas decorations to a crawl space over the rafters. I crouched in the shadows and waited, gazing down at the restaurant below me, smelling the aroma of fried chicken and potatoes, and letting the music wash over me. I had no idea until that moment that I could feel physically hungry for both food and music, but I was.

Hours passed by. Cops arrived and went. The CEDU enforcers came and went. The bartender shrugged. "Nope. "I haven't seen her."

Perched on a narrow board, I fought myself to stay awake to avoid falling. That was the hardest part. I felt so exhausted. Kyle was arriving from Los Angeles. It would take some time, but she was on her way, and we would drive quickly away from this shithole and into a town with a McDonald's. The waitress alternated between offering burgers and soup of the day. Oh my God, I was so hungry. She eventually chased the last of the late drinkers out of the bar, arranged chairs on the tables, and swept the floor, conversing with the cook as he cleaned the kitchen.

They switched off the lights and left.

Fuck my life.

Kyle would now be unable to get in. She was probably outside right now. I stretched my tight legs and crept down the steps. I put my ear against the door. Nothing. I opened it slightly and looked out into the silent parking lot. Moths flitted around the lights over the phone booth. I went to the pay phone to contact Kyle again. She accepted the accusations, and I said, "Kyle, where are you? Have you called the police?"

"No," she replied. "No, of course not."

A huge hand was clamped around my neck. I attempted to cling onto the phone, but the enforcer yanked me off the ground and shoved me into the SUV. They drove back to school, which was just about two or three miles away. I guess I was running in circles at times.

People were still at the Propheet event, looking like a pack of red-eyed zombies. Weaselmug appeared to be in the best mood of her life. She pulled me up in front of everyone and shouted, "Look who it is!"

I didn't notice the back of her hand coming at me. Next thing I knew, I was on the ground. An enforcer yanked me up, and they went berserk on me, punching and choking me and yelling at everyone to watch what happened. And everyone looked. Their eyes were the size of soccer balls. Many of them were crying. No question, this was an intense experience to behold, and I assume that was the objective. That is why they did not need barbed wire, steel bars, or iron doors. There was something far stronger keeping folks inside.

They told horror stories of dead children in the woods.

They had everyone ready to tell on everyone else.

They deceived those who care about you.

Aunt Kyle was in her twenties when this occurred. Not much older than me. We've never discussed it, but given her perspective at the time, how could she not call my mother? Her older sister. My parents did what you're supposed to do when your child disappears: they phoned the police. I was outraged when I was younger, but the more I learn about CEBU's brutally smart sales tactics, the more compassion I have for my family. They were really committed to doing the right thing for me at all times.

Consider this: based on the advice of a mental health specialist, you send your troubled child to this gorgeous boarding school that costs a fortune. When the kid tries to flee, do you believe the kid who has been causing you so much trouble? Or do you accept the psychiatrist who claims the child is a mad, unrepentant liar?

I am not the insane one; you are!—say 100 percent of insane individuals.

Local law enforcement frequently has financial ties with these places; they receive compensation for returning runaways and dismissing claims of abuse. And come on. Are there dead kids in the woods? That sounds like a B-movie plot.

Isn't it?

I mean, that cannot be true.

Or do we simply not want it to be real?

We don't want to believe that James Lee Crummel, a convicted child molester and serial killer who committed suicide in 2012 while on death row at San Quentin, was involved in a long string of horrific crimes, including the murders of two boys who went missing from CEDU's Running Springs campus in 1993 and 1994. According to Bill Gleason, a missing-person investigator for the Department of Justice, Crummel frequently accompanied visiting psychiatrist Dr. Burnell Forgey on excursions to CEDU. I'm not sure if Dr. Forgey is the same doctor that consulted with my parents, but he was there at the same time, convincing parents that their children needed to "work the program" for two years.

CHAPTER 8

THE CASCADE SCHOOL

I'm not sure what happened to Tess, but I spent the following few weeks pretending I was extremely sorry for running. I told Camo Goon that his beating had made me reflect on myself, and now all I wanted was to experience the life-changing greatness of Track/Trek. And I wasn't saying that because I expected another chance to run. They kept telling me I could go home after Track and Trek. They stated that was how you "graduated" from Ascent, and I believed them because the kids who went on the Track/Trek that Tess and I fled from had vanished.

"It's a beautiful moment," Burly stated. "You run that last bit, and when you get to the trailhead, your parents are there to celebrate with you."

I held on to that image—the moment I'd see Mom and Dad. At CEDU, I was constantly thinking of home, Nicky and my younger brothers, and how beautiful it was at the Waldorf. Now I've blocked it all out. It made me really sad. I worked my tail off for another chance at Track/Trek.

When the time came, I crushed the three-week hiking marathon, ascending and descending snow-covered mountains while carrying my eighty-pound bag. (Not exaggerating; they told us every day, "It's an eighty-pound pack, so use your legs when you lift.") We arrived at our encampment and built a sweat lodge—big branches lashed together into a roundhouse frame covered in canvas—before the camo squad led us in some twisted version of a supposedly Native American ritual.

The vision quest continued for days. We sat in a circle around a fire, only allowed to leave the sweat lodge to use the restroom—but we never had to use the restroom because we were given almost little food or water and were sweating furiously. We were not allowed to sleep for 72 hours. If a child passed out, we took them out into the snow to be revived before trudging back inside. It was our only source of cool air, so I sat there wishing for someone to pass out, even if it was myself.

We were all crying. Coughing. We're talking out of our skulls. My eyes and sinuses were burning from smoke and a lack of sleep. I heard the operator's voice.

Collect the call from Star. Will you accept the charges?

Collect the call from Star. Will you accept the charges?

And suddenly my head bobbed, startling me out of my half-sleep. I'm not sure why they forced us to chant, moan, howl, beat drums, and pass stones back and forth. I did not get it. It was beyond me. If there is a real Native American ritual in which all of these things symbolize something, please do not be offended. I am not disrespecting that. Not at all. I'm only saying that we were in no position to understand or appreciate anything like that, and the Camo Goons were not qualified to manage it.

Anyway, I toughed it out, focusing on the "home stretch" where Mom and Dad were waiting.

When I arrived, Burly was full of delight and happiness. "You got it, Paris! You've graduated!"

"I'm going home," I said. "Where are my parents?""

"They'll meet you in Redding and drive you to Cascade."

"The cascade. ..what . .."

"You've still got another year to work the program," she told you.

So—wow. Attempting to find words.

At that point, all that mattered was seeing Mom and Dad. I had to convince them that they were being manipulated by someone who was better at it than I was. Burly offered me some clothing, and I did my best to clean myself up, but I still felt dirty when I got into the car with Mom and Dad in Redding.

Dad looked sharp and well-groomed, as he always is. Mom smelled like a lavender patch in God's backyard. I just wanted to die with my head on her lap, while she stroked my hair and told me how glad she was to see me. When she brought up the alternative CEDU program, I begged and cried.

"Mom, please, please, please take me home."

"You'll like this place," she remarked. "Look. It's very lovely.

She gave me a leaflet with joyful pupils, verdant grass, and a stately lodge with a rainbow arcing across the sky above, along with the words The Cascade School.

For fucks sake.

"Mom, I can't," I said. "I am literally going through hell. These places are insane. These individuals are lying!"

"Let's not spend our time arguing," Mom added. "This is difficult for all of us. We need to be strong. We have one year left till you turn eighteen. This is our final chance to save you. "We must see it through."

"Could we perhaps make a halt somewhere? On the way to school, that is. There must be somewhere we can go. If I'm going to remain there for a year, I should at least have the roots highlighted so it can grow out without appearing completely jacked."

Mom consented, and we located a spot in Redding: a cute tiny salon in the hairstylist's home on the outskirts of town. Before we went inside, I hugged my father and told him, "I love you, Dad."

"I love you, Starry," he whispered, holding me close for a minute. "I hope you know we're only doing what's best for you."

I smiled at him and replied, "I know, Daddy."

Mom and I headed to the salon. I sat next to her until it was my turn, then I sat in my smock, smiling and chatting while the stylist covered up my roots.

"I need to use the restroom," I explained. "I'll be right back."

In the restroom, I ripped off my smock, shoved a magazine rack under the doorknob, and climbed out the window.

I ran like mad, removing the foils from my hair and stuffing them into my pockets. When I saw a Greyhound bus station, I dashed into the restroom. The bleach on my scalp smells strong and was beginning to sting, so I ducked my head into the tiny sink and cupped water over my burning scalp with my palm. I cleaned my hair as well as I could, ran my fingers through it, and twisted it into a tight bun on top of my head.

I examined the bus schedule and calculated how long it would take to go to Los Angeles while counting the money I'd taken from Mom's handbag. Even though it wasn't the most direct way, I boarded the first bus out and took a seat toward the back, slumped down below the edge of the window until the bus left town.

I believe the first stop was in Chico. A police officer stepped on and spoke briefly with the driver, who laughed and shook her head. The cop got off, and we drove on, never going as fast as I wanted. I hunched down, my heart thumping. I eventually fell asleep with my knees drawn up to my chest and my arms covering my head. I hadn't realized we'd stopped again until I felt a hard hand on my shoulder. I opened my eyes to see a cop standing there.

He responded: "I need you to come with me, Miss Hilton."

"Where is my mom?" "I want to talk to my mother."

"She's pretty upset," he explained. "One of the counselors from your school is here to take you back to campus."

I did not bother begging. I chose a woman who looked a lot like Weaselmug. Same mousy hair and forlorn countenance. We drove for about an hour, going through a dark forest of aromatic pine trees, across a frozen lake, and into the craggy mountains. We briefly halted before a large set of iron gates. There was a large rock with gold letters spelling CASCADE SCHOOL.

The main structure resembled a large wood home or lodge. They gave me a rulebook. Same CEDU arrangement as Running Springs: labor, monitored calls, rappers, and prophets. I felt nothing when the man counselor urged me to remove my garments. I squatted and coughed through the cavity search without whimpering. I slipped on my pinks and followed my new "big sister" into our room.

She turned out the lights, and I waited until she sounded asleep. Only then did I allow myself to touch the small roll of cash hidden beneath the bun on top of my head. The money was wrapped tightly, thin as a skeleton key.

See, I'd discovered that these strip searches were about invasion, not research. It was a display of their power over your entire body, so they concentrated on the private parts—the ones you naturally attempt to protect. Some of them clearly enjoyed it. They did not even bother faking. The cavity searches, like any sexual assault, were about the perpetrators rather than the victim. Once I realized it, it was simple to deceive them.

I devised a plan to keep my money hidden while I waited for my next opportunity to run. It was not a lot. A few hundred dollars. But it was mine. My precious little money rolls. Knowing it was there gave me a small burst of satisfaction. Money represents hope. Money represents freedom.

I resolved that someday I would work extremely hard and earn a lot of money. Like a million bucks. And then I will be safe and never trust anyone again.

I spent my days at Cascade working on a construction job, hoping not to be recognized. Weeks passed by. Perhaps one month. One day when we were gathering rocks, a thin little girl approached me. I can't recall her name; in my imagination, she was always Mouse.

"Are you going to run?""She whispered."

I did not say anything. Did not look at her.

"Take me with you," Mouse requested. "If I stay here, I'll die."

Fuck.

She was very slender and small—only up to my shoulder, perhaps fourteen—and she wept a lot. She kept getting ripped apart in Raps for "tempting" her uncle and forcing him to do evil things. She hadn't figured it out yet; you needed to distract them. For example, "Oh, I hate myself because everyone in my family is vegetarian, and I used to sneak out to Burger King." Let them all jump on that. "Bitch! Animal eaters! Cow Murderer!" Who cares if people make you cry over something that isn't true? I mean, it's annoying. It still hurts. However, it is not as horrible as people pounce on the actual you. If they get their hooks into something real, guilt consumes you from within, and you become your own worst enemy. (Use as needed with internet trolls and gossip blogs.)

"Please, take me with you," Mouse asked. "Please."

Crap. This complicated matters, but I couldn't leave her, knowing what it was like to be left behind, and knowing that the lady with the long black braid would have responded "of course" and assisted her without question. I wanted to be like her, not like the others who turned away.

Mouse and I went running one night while the moon was shining brightly. I carried her down the hillside, holding her tiny wrist in my palm. No compassion. There's no stopping. We needed to get back to the Greyhound terminal. That was the only way out.

Finally, I spotted a 7-Eleven.

Gotta adore 7-Eleven. Open all night. Now it was almost morning.

"We need a disguise," I informed Mouse.

I was watching my spending, but I got some cheap brown mascara and used it to thicken our brows into heavy unibrows. I feathered my mustaches and even gave myself a thin goatee. We slicked our hair back beneath baseball caps and hoodies from the bargain bin and boarded a Greyhound bus, aiming to walk like beat boys. (Honestly, thinking about that makes me laugh now.) We sat down in our seats and remained silent throughout the lengthy, twisting ride. We arrived in Los Angeles about ten or twelve hours later and disappeared into the metropolis.

My friend graciously allowed us to stay at his Bel Air home, which is only a few minutes from the Jaclyn Smith house where I grew up. I spent the first few days sleeping, eating, and listening to music. Mouse and I spent hours in front of the television, soaking up everything we'd missed. When it felt safe to go out, I headed to the Whiskey Bar at the Sunset Marquis Hotel, which is where all the rock stars stay. I sat in the corner, bobbing my head to the Cardigans' "Lovefool." I sang loudly and joyfully. I felt protected and alive, despite being lost in the crowd.

Love me, tell me you love me.

Fool me, fool me. ..Hey—off topic, but not really—have you seen Repo? What about the Genetic Opera?

In 2006, I wanted to try something absolutely different. Twisted Pictures' producer Mark Burg approached me with the strangest proposal I'd ever heard: an immense, gruesome, grand rock opera in the style of Tommy, The Black Parade, or Quadrophenia. Think Saw meets Moulin Rouge.

Repo! The Genetic Opera is set in a dystopian universe where the human population is plagued by genetic organ failure, forcing people to buy transplant organs, and if they can't pay, the organs are repossessed by the wicked slasher Repo Man, who is actually just a father attempting to protect his daughter Shilo. Meanwhile, Rottissimo, the merciless megarich giant who dominates this nightmarish planet, learns that he is dying and must decide which of his warped children will inherit his money and power: vicious Luigi, psychotic Pavi, or beauty-obsessed Amber Sweet.

I spent several weeks studying the script and working on the music with Roger Love, the vocal coach, who described how being frightened causes that baby voice that I can't seem to shake. I auditioned for Mark and the director, Darren Lynn Bousman, who had produced and directed three Saw films, and they wanted me to play Amber Sweet. It was a privilege to collaborate with Paul Sorvino (Mira's father, Goodfellas, etc.) as Rottissimo and Sarah Brightman (Phantom of the Opera) as Blind Mag, who gouges out her own eyes and is impaled on a fence. It's that type of scene.

The screenplay called for Amber Sweet to sing her face off—literally sing until her face tears off the front of her head—so I'd have to keep working with the vocal coach every day and spend hours in the chair getting prosthetics and makeup done. Several sick looks designed by

Alex Kavanagh take Amber Sweet on a transforming journey from Rottissimo's bratty little girl to a raging transplant addict who swaps sex for surgery.

Following a limited theatrical release, the film was made available on DVD. There was a special screening at Comic-Con in 2010, and strangely, it performed exceptionally well in the Czech Republic. Lionsgate handled distribution, and the picture carved out a small place for itself as a campy cult favorite beloved by many of the same fans of The Rocky Horror Picture Show. Goth girls dressed up like Amber Sweet for Halloween. I connected with a completely new fan base. I am quite proud of the vocal moments I discovered in the music. This soundtrack was wild, featuring Rob Zombie, Guns N' Roses, and Slipknot's Shawn "Clown" Crahan. We had so much fun on set. Lots of great recollections.

Repo! is mostly a narrative about fathers and daughters.

One plot is about a loving guy who takes a bad decision: to protect his frail daughter, he imprisons her in a dark house. ("She's been caged up like a monster by her overbearing father," the narrator sings.) The second plotline is about a dreadful man who makes a compassionate choice: in order to empower his broken daughter, he sacrifices his own vision of how her life should be.

In the Spirograph of memory and understanding, I realize that my father and I represent both stories.

Fathers and daughters. It's a challenging dynamic. I don't know anyone who has gotten it completely on either side. Finally, We the Daughters must recognize that a father is more than the sum of his most difficult decisions. I don't doubt my father's affection for me. I hope he understands how much I adore him, how grateful I am for his wisdom and assistance, and how much I value his part in our family's genetic opera.

CHAPTER 9

THAT WAS SO ME

The year 1998 was essentially a black hole in my life—no music, no television, no knowledge of significant advancements in communication and technology, or anything else going on in the world. In January 1999, I graduated from Provo Canyon School, and Britney Spears released her debut album. ..Baby, one more time. I couldn't have enough. The rebellious spirit. A novel way to mix and edit music. On that record, she wears the music like a catsuit. I was dying to know how they accomplished it. The technological difference may not have been as evident to some, but I had been music-deprived for the majority of the previous two years.

The video for the title track is now online. ..Britney sits in class, flipping her pencil and bouncing her foot as the agonizing seconds pass. Then the doorbell rings. She's free.

That impatient schoolgirl is dying to be free. Then she is. And she morphs into herself. I liked the idea of a girl being able to embrace her sensual side and enjoy it without feeling shame or fear. But then there's that recurring line: "My loneliness is killing me." Because a female who doesn't comply, who is defiant and daring, who demonstrates her strength and sexuality—that girl is on her own, no matter how many boys dangle from her charm bracelet.

For two years, I was ravenous for music, art, and food—everything that made life beautiful or even bearable—but most of all, I was hungry for love. Since the night I crawled out the window to kiss the pedophile, I've felt disconnected from my family. That was the most horrific element of what I had gone through. We were divided by layers of shame, falsehoods, and denial rather than actual distance.

To be a good "graduate," you were meant to claim that CEDU and

Provo saved your life. They conditioned us to believe that if we talked shit about the school, the school would talk even worse shit about us—to our families, potential jobs, and, in my case, the tabloids. It was a powerful muzzle. Most survivors, including myself, wanted to go on with our lives and never think about those locations again.

I recently asked another victim, "How did you deal with things in the first year after Provo?"" and she added, "I drank until I went blind."

Self-medication is prevalent among survivors. Self-harm is also an option. It makes complete sense. It takes a lot of effort to fake it in a world you no longer recognize, and advanced imaging shows that childhood trauma affects the brain: the nucleus accumbens, the pleasure center where addiction takes over; the prefrontal cortex, where impulse control occurs—or does not occur; and the amygdala, where fear lives.

Nicky, the bright-yellow pool noodle, saved me from drowning during my first few months of freedom. While I was gone, she had progressed beyond the knobby, pony-legged stage that tall girls go through in junior high. At fifteen, she landed a lovely internship at a prominent fashion magazine and dreamed of starting her own design empire. Elegance radiated from her complexion, hands, feet, chin set, and every other aspect of her. She possessed Dad's thin stature and Mom's impeccable social skills. Nicky always knew what was proper to do, and she did it without being prissy or false. She knew how to pull it off. She has a wild side, but her overall attitude is sensible, classic virtue with a cool intelligence edge—like Audrey Hepburn in Funny Face.

Nicky grew up in a typical, supportive environment. She excelled at Sacred Heart's healthy school environment, learned from exposure to New York's exclusive social scene, and slept in a quiet room where she felt cherished and protected. I was not jealous of my sister, but I was envious. While I was tied up, Nicky and I traded places; she marched forward while I stood still—or was dragged backward. When I got out of Provo, she was very protective of me, and I looked up to her, as if she had become the big sister and I was the little sister, always trying to catch up. I still feel this way today.

I wasn't surprised to learn that Nicky and my younger brothers, aunts and uncles, grandparents, family friends, and even Wendy White, who always knew everything, had no idea where I was between the summer of 1997 and January 1999. Mom, Dad, and I had a nasty little secret. We did not discuss it. It was as if the past seventeen months never occurred.

Mom had a long convoluted story that I heard in parts and pieces from friends, hairdressers, and anyone else who puzzled why I left so totally and reappeared so soon. Someone called to interview her for a magazine piece, and when they refused to accept her ambiguous comments, she went into prank-call mode.

"Paris and Nicky interviewed at Sacred Heart. Nicky is going to graduate. It has been a lovely experience for her. But Paris responded, 'Mom, no way am I going to an all-girls school.' So she went to the performing arts high school, where she had a 3.8 GPA. She's really intelligent. But you know how it is with dedicated ballerinas, and—well, she went to Dwight and didn't bond with anyone there. Teachers. Students. It was just. .."

She grimaced and held the phone in her fist.

"Run away?" Of course, she didn't run away. That's just one of those crazy things. ..no. There was a stalker. "Stalking her."

(The stalker aspect was true; that actually happened.)

"It was the most terrifying thing I've ever experienced. Here's a lovely female being followed. Being stalked. We were receiving weird mail. We did everything to keep her safe. It was her senior year, thus she graduated from homeschooling. In London. So, in addition to Waldorf security, we now have private security following them around, monitoring their every move. We see everything. "Who, what, where, and when?"

I took my lead from Mom and stuck with that story. I was delighted to portray her and Dad as alert, fully present parents. That was who they wanted to be. That is who they are: parents willing to go to any length for their children. Only in my instance, they ended up on the wrong end.

I had lost my sense of self around them. I was walking on eggshells, trying to say what I felt they wanted to know. Pigface had warned me that even after I graduated from Provo High, my parents may send me to a mental hospital at any time. I didn't believe it at the time, but years later, when I witnessed Britney's situation—how her father officially took control of her personal and professional life—it shook me. My parents made every effort to reintegrate me into the family dynamic, but certain lessons are unbreakable. Underscoring everything they did to show me how much they loved me, my keepers at CEDU, Ascent, and Provo instilled in me the following idea: They sent you away. They could not stand you. You are an embarrassment to everyone you love. That message was played on repeat like the jagged edge of a jigsaw, carving a deep groove.

In my opinion, love is conditional and cannot be trusted. Love was something I didn't deserve, but I could control if I kept a safe distance.

My little brothers were both humorous and lovely. Barron was ten now and ecstatic to see me. He just wanted to hang out with me at the park; he didn't know many other adult(ish) people who were willing to ride the swings, slides, and teeter-totter with him. Conrad was five and had a lot of questions about bugs, animals, space, and science. They were both bright and cute. I adored them, but there was a void in those relationships that we would have to fill over time.

When there is a significant age difference between the oldest and youngest members of a family, it is almost as if the families are completely distinct. But it was more than that. Conrad had no recall of what happened before I moved in with Gram Cracker. Between Palm Springs and CEDU, I was a chaos agent, constantly in confrontation with my parents. Now I was back, and the strain was like a constant ringing in my ear. I didn't want to be separated from my family again, but the moment I stepped into my family's apartment at the Waldorf, I knew I couldn't stay.

I was scared to sleep in the room where I had been taken. I sat up doodling and sketching, listening to music, making lists, and thinking about how to generate money and utilize the advantages no one could take away from me: my face, name, legs, modeling contacts, and runway experience—none of which would mean anything if I wasn't willing to work hard. And I was willing. I knew I could work as a rock hauler.

I tried briefly to complete high school at Canterbury, a Catholic boarding school in New Milford, Connecticut. They did not abuse children—well done, Canterbury!—But Catholic school did not work for me. One positive thing: I got to play ice hockey. As a child, I used to love going to the Rockefeller Center skating rink. I was quick and ferocious on the rink. Now I have a lot of aggressiveness to work out, and hockey is ideal for that. I flew around, waving my large stick. I appreciated the fresh, cold air in the arena, as well as the fresh, cool girls on the team.

I made a few fun pals who were willing to join me and go clubbing. Normally, we rode the metro into town, but one night, I treated us all to a limo. I requested the guy to wait outside campus, but he showed up like, "Yes, I'm here for Paris Hilton." This was not well welcomed. And it was the final straw. I had been skipping classes and failing everything, so they kicked me out.

In 2007, Canterbury's director of finance informed the Danbury News-Times that "her goals and priorities were not the goals and priorities of the school."

I agree with that.

I went to Storm King, a beautiful institution for rich fucked-up kids, but I was kicked out for the typical reasons, including keeping ferrets beneath my bed. My final choice was Beekman, a small school a few blocks from the Waldorf, and I was so bored that I said, "Forget this."

There was nothing wrong with any of these places, but I had exactly zero transferable credits after ninth grade in Palm Springs. This was a shocking awakening for my parents, who had brought into CEDIs "integrated arts and academics" promise. CEDU held an elaborate "graduation" ceremony in which bogus diplomas were distributed; Provo Canyon did not bother. So, at the age of eighteen, I'd have to enroll in tenth grade at any properly approved high school, public or private.

Hard pass.

I began learning my way around the recording studio in the same way. I met a producer who had previously worked with Jessica Simpson and Kelly Rowland, and we collaborated on the early tracks that would later become my debut album. The studio was bliss for me, combining two things I adore nearly as much as my own skin: music and technology. The migration of music into the computer world is something we take for granted now, yet it was a time of great freedom and empowerment. Creators no longer need permission; before GarageBand and Logic Pro, there was only Logic—democratizing software that opened the garage door and allowed everyone in.

The paparazzi were advancing with digital cameras and lightweight video equipment that allowed them to capture arable walk-and-talk film footage as well as clearer, higher-definition images in almost all lighting conditions. Going out practically every night in Los Angeles and New York, I received a lot of attention, which I enjoyed. It made me feel like a superstar. After a lengthy period of not being able to gaze in a mirror, I relished feeling lovely.

Instead of cursing or dodging the photographers, as many people did, I waved and shouted, "Hey, boys!"" They made sure they captured all the wonderful angles of me fighting with my shopping bags, having frozen yogurt, and looking like Marilyn Monroe on the train grate. They could get paid more for candid photographs. Unlike a red carpet, where dozens of photographers capture essentially the same image, the candid images were distinct. Tabloids desired photographs of celebrities in candid moments, such as eating a burger or walking the dog, as if they were actual people. The paparazzi were not permitted to enter a club and disturb patrons, so they camped outside, waiting for us to emerge.

I bought some gorgeous sneakers from a small shop on Melrose. When you pressed the side button, roller skates appeared from the bottom. These were my favorite club shoes of all time. I zipped all over the place. If a forceful guy hit on me, I dashed across the dance floor. It made for wonderful video as I zoomed up and down the street, in and out of parties and nightclubs. People began dubbing me "Roller Girl," which I enjoyed. They could have been talking to the Roller Girl porn star from Boogie Nights, but the film came out when I was at Ascent, so I didn't know about it until years later.

I was having a good time, but I was also contributing significantly.

Why shouldn't I get paid to attend that party and promote that brand?

It's kind of funny to me when people think I put myself out there because I wanted attention like a pound puppy. I enjoyed feeling unique, of course, but I began earning real money when I learned I was an amplifier and attention was the power cord. I turned attention into a valuable commodity to help brands I believed in, including my own. I was always aware, on some level, that there was a distinction between that kind of attentiveness and love. However, when love did not come along, the incessant clicking served as an adequate substitute.

Carter and his brother, Courtney, co-authored the book Shortcut Your Startup: Speed Up Success with Unconventional Advice from the Trenches (Gallery Books, 2018) before we met. If that book had been available when I initially began developing my businesses—oh, wait. Never mind. I would not have read it. I wasn't much into reading books. Now, I'm a bit of a business book addict. I have Carter bring an extra carry-on so I may shop in the airport bookshop before my trip. Back then, I was simply living my life moment by moment, but I was doing things that had not yet been invented, such as taking selfies. I didn't pause to consider what to term it or whether it made up to some sort of strategy.

Anyway, Accelerate Your Startup.

In their book, Carter and Courtney pose "three key questions before you start anything":

What does success look like to you?

Why hasn't anyone else done this?

Why are you? Why now?

Looking back, I didn't even realize I was beginning up.

For me, success was a magnificent ballet of security, respect, and the potential to serve others. I wanted to secure my freedom, show the world what I was capable of, and support businesses and artists I believed in. That is still how I define success. My primary goal has never changed, and while it does include making as much money as possible, it has never been about money for its own reason. It's always been about how I wanted to feel, not what I wanted to achieve.

I believe no one else has ever done what I did, because no one has ever been me before: a special girl born in the dawn of the Age of Aquarius, with my unique combination of privileges that pulled me up and disadvantages that forced me to mature. I'm sure I wasn't the first socialite to calculate the party equation, but my experience and determination allowed me the courage to ask. Making the ask is where many business ventures fail. Pride gets in the way. Or the cliched "that's not how it's always been done." My pride had been shattered, and I didn't know or care how things had been done before. I was doing everything I could to burn my history to the ground. So I made the request, and as Jesus said, "Ask and it shall be given unto you."

Why me? Because I did not trust anyone else. And why now? Because this is all there is. Now is all that matters. This could just be my ADHD talking, but this is the only universe worth living in.

On New Year's Eve 1999, I celebrated like—well, you know.

Some others were horrified by the prospect of Y2K, but I happily flipped the page. New year, decade, and century. Accepting the assumption that this would be my finest millennium yet, I embarked on a life of relentless work and travel that would last for the following two decades.

CHAPTER 10

THE FIRST STEP TO SELF-REINVENTION

I turned nineteen in February 2000. I recognized what I had going for me, which was a lot. I was strong. I was gorgeous. I could make people laugh. I knew where to go and how to be visible. I joined a major modeling agency, continued to expand my side business—getting paid to party—and began paying more attention to debates about real estate and investing. It was an eventful time for Hilton International. There was discussion of a hotel on the moon, but Papa was still the chairman of the board, and his feet remained firmly on the ground. Hilton has bought Doubletree, Hampton, Homewood, and Embassy Suites. They already had Bally's and Caesars in Las Vegas.

I told Papa, "I think I want to have my own hotels someday."

Most people would have looked at me like I was proposing a hotel on the moon, but my grandfather said, "Of course." "You should definitely do that." He didn't offer to assist me, but he and Dad answered my inquiries and guided me through some initial interactions. I knew I needed a manager, but I wasn't sure who to trust aside from Dad and Papa. I despised the idea of giving up a portion of my profits, so I created a fictitious manager with her own email address and harsh, smokey voice on the phone.

"Yes, I received your offer and confirmed Miss Hilton's availability." If we can compromise on the back-end % and add an extra $10,000 up front, I believe we have a deal. "Yes, I will fax you her signature."

I don't remember the false manager's name, but she reminded me of an older Amber Taylor. She negotiated for me like a pit bull. Even after I signed with a major modeling agency, I kept her on for odd assignments.

In May 2000, I attended the Cannes Film Festival for the first time. I brought entirely too much luggage with me because every day featured at least three or four looks: a breezy walk around town bumping into movie stars, tasteful lazing by the pool like Marilyn Monroe, and a spectacular evening out at the art film look. I worked hard to perfect my look for a lunch date with one of Hollywood's most influential guys. I wanted Harvey Weinstein to see a lady who belonged in the business: sophisticated, beautiful, casting-worthy, and distinct from all the other nineteen-year-old ladies with huge movie star fantasies. I was with a producer friend who was pitching a concept. This was a fantastic chance for both of us, and we wanted to make the right impression.

The lunch wasn't a success. The producer sat there squirming and saying nothing as Harvey made pervy, strange remarks about me and my potentially lucrative career in his world. He was as creepy and aggressive as anyone could be during lunch in a packed restaurant. We departed with little optimism for my friend's initiative.

The following night, I attended an amfAR (American Foundation for AIDS Research) event. Harvey saw me across the room and yelled out to me; I pretended I didn't notice him and moved away. He followed me.

I walked faster.

He walked faster.

I went to the ladies' room with my unicorn trot and locked myself in a stall before he arrived. He hammered on the stall door and yanked on the doorknob, saying nasty, drunk crap like "Ya wanna be a star?" while I was locked inside, thinking, Where the fuck is a bathroom window when you need one? Until the French security guards entered and forced him out of the ladies' room. He yelled, "This is my event!" "I'm Harvey Weinstein." But they didn't understand—or cared—and actually hauled him outside.

I didn't tell anyone, because that's what you did back then. It was similar to the bucket shower: if you wanted to survive, you simply accepted it. Years later, when the scandal broke and the Weinstein power structure began to disintegrate, reporters repeatedly asked me, "Have you ever had a Harvey Weinstein thing?"

And I said, "Nope."

It made me feel ashamed, and I suffer from a compulsive dread of being embarrassed. I was scared that if I told the incident, the following inquiry would be, "Why didn't you speak up at the time?" I had no answer to that. That is one of those inquiries that shifts the guilt to someone who should not have to bear it.

This: "Why didn't you scream?"

Or: "Why didn't you kick him in the balls?"

The only answer to these inquiries is, "Why don't you go fuck yourself?" I respect the brave ladies who stood up and confronted him, but every woman who has gone through something with him—and others like him—has the right to process it in the way that works best for her. No woman should be ashamed of taking care of herself.

That year, in Cannes, the Palme d'Or went to Björk's film Dancer in the Dark, about a factory worker who is going blind. At a sad point in the film, she explains, "I've got little games that I play when things get very hard... "I just start dreaming, and everything becomes music."

That's a fantastic assessment of my coping abilities back then. And now.

I was walking a lot of red carpets, feeling long-legged and strong, and developing my own style. After missing a pivotal year of pop culture and style impact, I had no choice but to create my own. It made me feel insecure, which was unnecessary because establishing your own style is liberating. If you follow the crowd, it's too late; whoever blazed that road has moved on, so you might as well blaze your own, even if others don't comprehend it.

Fashion reporters constantly praised my "distinctive walk" on the runway—some loved it, others despised it—but I had no idea what that meant. When I look back at photos from the first two years after Provo, I feel a burden on my shoulders. My stance reflected a lot of rage, hurt, and embarrassment. I suppose it came across as nonchalance. Coolness. No fucks were given. But it was actually a girl's walk, which was often interrupted by her need to catch up with herself.

We danced to "The Real Slim Shady" with a sweeping one-arm wave, the flat refrain repeating with the strobe lights: "Please stand up."

In my perspective, it was a song about imposterhood—the fact that we all pretended to be tough—the only thing we had in common.

One night, Nicky and I were singing karaoke in a club when we spotted a guy staring at us. He was hot—or maybe he just radiated the confidence that makes people think you're hot. If you believe in your heart that you are hot, you are hot, according to the rules of hotness physics.

This person was older than me. Coarse. Arrogant. The overconfident "bad boy" from Central Casting, the ideal guy for a girl experiencing the most self-destructive period of her life. I wasn't looking for Mr. Right, but Mr. Spite. He adored his nickname, "Scum." That struck me as extremely badass.

We started dating, and I must admit that he was just as charming as Mr. Abercrombie. It was all incredibly thrilling and naughty—an entirely new type of adrenaline. I was obsessed.

I don't recall much from the night he wanted to record a videotape of us making love. He had frequently stated that it was something he did with other women, but I felt strange and uncomfortable about it. I constantly told him that I couldn't. It's really embarrassing."

He continued pressing. I kept making excuses: I was tipsy and exhausted after a long night of partying. The lighting wasn't ideal. My hair and makeup were wonderful. He said I always looked beautiful no matter what, and it didn't matter because this wasn't a show. It was only for us. Nobody else would ever see it. And then he said that if I didn't do it, he could simply find someone who would, which was the worst thing I could imagine—being rejected by this grown man because I was a stupid kid who didn't know how to play grown-up games.

The truth is that I wanted to be alive in a sensual sense. I wanted to feel like a lady who is confident in her own skin. I was struggling to comprehend my sexuality and couldn't have explained it to anyone else. I had no words for it. I had never heard the term asexual.

I understand, right?

The world sees me as a sex symbol, and I welcome that since symbol literally means icon. But when people saw the sex footage, they said slut, not icon. They said "whore." They were not shy about it. The irony is that I avoided sex as a result of the violence and degradation I experienced as an adolescent, and possibly also because of how I was raised. I despised the notion of sex. I avoided sex until it was completely unavoidable.

I needed to prove something to him and myself, so I went drunk and did it.

Despite the age difference and the difficulties of my high-mileage work life, I had a relationship with this guy on and off for a couple of years—a long period for a teenage girl. I eventually became bored and pissed him off. My girlfriends and I went to karaoke one night and met Nicolas Cage, who asked us to an after-party. We didn't go since it was Nicolas Cage. We would have attended an after-party at Billy Bob Nobody's place just as easily. Because of the afterparty! Bring it. So we went to this house with a car and a motorcycle in the living room, as well as a collection of shrunken heads upstairs, and everyone had a nice time.

When I returned to my residence, my on/off lover was there, furious that I hadn't returned his calls. There was a bit of drama, but that was it. This is how most of my relationships have ended over the years. I despise confrontations, so I always attempted to avoid the person. Sometimes they get the message. They did become angry at times. This was not the ugliest scene to arise from that MO. For a long time, I assumed that if someone became so jealous that they flung a phone at your head or grabbed you and shook you till your neck bones rattled, it must imply they genuinely loved you, right?

Ugh.

A few days after the shrunken-head party, a woman approached me at a club and tossed a glass of red wine in my face, which was an odd coincidence. I'm not sure what that was about. I had already moved on.

That videotape was never in my thoughts.

Why would it?

Back then, there was no YouTube, so an average individual couldn't submit something like that on the internet. The technology to humiliate someone on that level had not yet been devised.

On New Year's Eve 2000, I traveled to Vegas and bought many

small animals, including two ferrets and a baby goat. When I arrived at the airport with all of these pet boxes and supplies, the gate agent informed me, "This is not a traveling zoo." I had to charter a limo and drive through ten hours of New Year's Eve traffic back to Los Angeles by myself, with my new animal companions crapping all over the seats. I spent the first several hours of 2001 drinking champagne and helping the driver clean up.

Thus, the aughts were labeled as the decade of excess.

CHAPTER 11

SMILE AT THE CAMERA

I preferred the early 2000s party feel to the late 1990s; you were encouraged to be outgoing and extravagant. What Not to Wear premiered in 2003, and Fashion Police debuted in 2010, when Twitter had stifled everyone's ability to think independently. I'm not sure why there hasn't been an exhibition highlighting truly unique and individual style, but you know what? You do not need permission to become an icon.

Madonna wears tulle skirts with motorcycle boots.

Sarah Jessica Parker wears circular skirts and fascinators.

Gaga wears elevator boots and a butcher dress.

Someone had to do it first, correct? It doesn't matter if the people around you don't get it right now; one of the benefits of the internet is that the moment is preserved indefinitely. In 2001, Björk was mocked for wearing a Marjan Pejoski swan dress to the Oscars. It is now iconic.

Naturally, the contrary is also true. The unpleasant moments also live on and are likely to receive more retweets. However, the key is to wear whatever makes you feel good. When I offer looks, ideas, and goods as an influencer, my goal is not to teach you how to satisfy others, but to encourage you to please yourself. Even if the appearance does not last, the memory of that pleasant feeling will. And who knows. When the time comes, the look may go through a transformation. Papa used to remark, "Even a broken clock is right twice a day." Style travels round and around: Spirograph, not etch-a-sketch.

I moved into a large house with two other females, Playboy bunnies

Jennifer Rovero and Nicole Lenz, who were always ready to party and had standing invitations to whatever was going on at the Playboy Mansion. We each had our own floor, which included large bedrooms, bathrooms, and walk-in closets. The mid-century modern wallpaper and furnishings (boomerang coffee tables, papasan chairs, and glass bricks) reminded me of Austin Powers: The Spy Who Shagged Me. We dubbed the landlord Mr. Furley after the somewhat spooky elderly landlord played by Don Knotts in Three's Company.

The area was calm and full of flowers, making it an ideal home base for me. You don't find a house like that in Los Angeles at the price we could afford, so we couldn't believe our luck. We were like, "Oh, my God!" How are we able to rent such a large house for so little? Then we discovered Mr. Furley wasn't leaving. We moved in, and he remained in his room on the top floor. That was the catch. He insisted he wasn't spying on us, and we saw no evidence of it, but we believed he might have had peepholes.

But it was an absolutely fantastic home!

Obviously, this would not be acceptable for any nineteen-year-old girl today, but Jen and Nicole were a couple of years older than me and perfectly secure in their own skin. They had extensive expertise dealing with a variety of difficult situations. They didn't enjoy Mr. Furley haunting the place, but it wasn't a deal breaker. We believed we could keep a watch on Mr. Furley, and as long as he didn't try anything, it was worth giving him the impression that he was Hugh Hefner's Mini-I live in a house with a group of gorgeous girls. And he never attempted anything.

To be honest, I didn't care. It's unfortunate, but I was essentially conditioned to being seen naked. I'd want to say it was because I was given free and complete control over my body, but the truth is that modesty was another thing I'd been denied. Modesty was a luxury I learnt to live without. How else could anyone tolerate the invasive shower observation day after day? Some girls died slowly within. Not me. I simply become numb to it. After a while, the offensive comments simply bounced off the wall. When they looked at me with their slimy little eyes, I glared back, thinking, "Eat your heart out, fuckface."

Creepy behavior is about the creeper, not the one being creeped on.

The mind has strong coping mechanisms; practically anything may be normalized or compartmentalized if the alternative is to go insane. I'm not saying it was great, but it made me stronger and forced me to get past how other people perceived me. After going through that, I was tough enough to take whatever the online trolls threw at me. You cannot internalize the hatred, judgment, and degraded Twitspew. It is a poisonous wild berry cooler of garbage that paralyzes you and gives the anonymous complete control.

These days, I truly feel empowered by having complete control over my body, but this is something I developed over time. It took me years to realize that I'm a performance artist, and my body is my medium—like a blank canvas or an empty stage—and that I won't be able to create anything important if I approach the job with shame and timidity. It's not about how much skin you show; it's about who controls the situation.

Modeling and acting require you to be comfortable with being stared at—even objectified—but you must accept it. You're not there as a prop for someone else's art; you're there as a collaborator, bringing a shared vision to life and propelling that idea to new heights thanks to your own creative contributions. Nobody has the right to take it somewhere you don't wish to go. The greatest photographers realize this. They motivate you to go above and beyond by including you in the vision.

This was before the iPhone, but I kept my old beeper with me at all times to take advantage of any possibilities that arose. One day, I received a request to assist with an ad campaign for Iceberg jeans. It paid well, and the photographer was David LaChapelle. This was enormous.

David was Andy Warhol's protégé when he was a teenager, therefore my parents knew him back then. When his first book, LaChapelle Land, was published in 1996, New York magazine dubbed him "the Fellini of photography" because he sparked outrage with photographs that literally microwaved everything you ever thought about constructions like beauty, art, and odd. Naked people packed into a Plexiglas box. Children are wrecking a posh dinner party. The settings are vivid and distinctive.

David has a distinct style, similar to that of Herb Ritts, Annie Leibovitz, and Richard Avedon. You identify his work as soon as you see it. I'd never seen anything like the photographs LaChapelle was taking back then. The faces are stunning. No fear, hesitancy, or constraint. I wanted to feel what they were feeling. I wished to be a work of art like that.

David simply wanted someone who was available. That morning, they had set up the Iceberg shoot only to realize that the model he had picked did not suit the designer's sample sizes. So he beeped at me. It was weird for a minute since I'd been out partying every night that week—dancing my ass off at a succession of parties and raves, living on catnaps and French fries—but I wasn't going to pass up this opportunity. I zipped over from my place in Los Angeles, making sure to avoid my mother, showered, dressed, and got myself together in record time. I arrived at the shoot forty-five minutes after he beeped at me. I was dying with excitement.

Everything went perfectly. Nothing excessive. He worked on a lot of regular commercial campaigns back then, including this one. Cool, yet suited for a general readership in print.

I wanted to be in one of David LaChapelle's classic shoots with the weird setups that feel like stills from an NC-17 art-house film that only existed in his head. Participating in those images was not just modeling; it was performance art. I was glad for the opportunity to show him how hard I was willing to work, and I hoped it would lead somewhere.

His second novel, Hotel LaChapelle (Bulfinch, 1999), recreated Madonna as Krishna, Leonardo DiCaprio as Marlon Brando, and Marilyn Manson as a school security guard. He posed as Barbie holding a small gun, shooting Ewan McGregor in the face as he broke into her Dream House.

That book came out shortly after I left Provo. As I relearned New York, I noticed it in every bookshop window, and I tried not to dwell on the possibility that I might have been there if I hadn't vanished. I wondered if he'd heard about the London boarding school, or if he'd even noticed I was gone.

I try not to remember how effortlessly I slipped through a fissure in the floor. It's as if you were going down the street with your pals and one of them slipped under an open manhole, you'd notice, right? I sure would! I mean...I believe I would. I hope I will. Perhaps we're all so focused straight ahead that folks slip away when we're not looking.

Shit. Let's all take a moment to check on our people. Make sure no one has fallen down a manhole.

I apologize if I didn't notice you slipped down a manhole. And if you didn't notice when I slipped down the manhole, please know I'm not upset about it.

Anyway, I caught up with David at a party and told him I'd love to work with him again. (Networking is always networking.) I didn't tell him everything that happened to me during my lost years, but he could tell there was a lot. I believe this is a significant component of his genius. He sees. I wonder if he realized we had something in common: we'd both suffered some injury in our teens.

We discussed Andy Warhol's muse, Edie Sedgwick, the fascinating concept of the "It Girl," and how celebrity worship resembles religious rapture.

For three generations, the Hilton men were the power players, while the Hilton ladies were either show horses or "behind every man there's a good woman" women. They had their own interests and deep inner lives, but above all, they were Mrs. Hilton. Nicky and I were expected to marry respectable men and carry on the old customs. My brothers were expected to marry nice ladies and carry on the Hilton name.

And then there's me.

Before his death, Papa liked to joke, "I spent the majority of my life as Conrad Hilton's son." "Now I am Paris Hilton's grandfather."

Those David LaChapelle photographs represent the tipping point at which all of history shifted into the future. They created a deluge of opportunities for me, propelling my name from tabloids to A-list status above and beyond the gossip industry. I progressed from model to supermodel, appearing in important New York Fashion Week presentations. My side hustle, getting paid to party, has grown into a real income. Like, a lot of cash. The more people saw me, the more money I made—not only for myself, but also for others around me.

All of this happened during the dot-com renaissance. Perez Hilton claims he started blogging in the early 2000s "because it seemed easy." And it was. The internet was a giant black hole that absorbed every piece of content it could find. Suddenly, all these eyeballs were out there, with no restrictions on what you might show them.

Celebrity gossip was the new information age's equivalent of the Chicken McNugget: not particularly nutritious but tasty. And irresistible.

I was at the center of that perfect storm.

"We've always had the celebrated ones," David explained, but this was different. People didn't start using the term "influencer" until 2015, so I had no idea what it was or what it would become when it started. I didn't know what else to do but live my life, for better or worse, so I just kept doing it as everything grew larger than life.

You probably remember what occurred next.

Paris Hilton happened.

CHAPTER 12

HIT THE GROUND

Facebook debuted in February 2004, and I kept hearing about it, but it was primarily for college students.

"Don't take it personally," Nicky said, and I didn't, but it was a bizarre reminder that there was once a little girl named Star who wanted to be a veterinarian. But I didn't attend college. People who were hired to educate me failed, so I had to educate myself by doing, dreaming, and experimenting, reading and listening, messing things up and mending them again. I had to scavenge for my education from the all-you-can-eat buffet of life. My self-education is a collection of experiences held together by towering role models.

Again: I was born into luxury. I'm not downplaying that. But I could have coasted, and I never did. I worked. And if my life went apart, I worked harder. One priceless bit of advice my great-grandfather gave my grandfather, and my grandfather gave me: "Success is never final. Failure is never fatal."

I have seen both up close.

Anyway, No college. So no Facebook for me in 2004. Perhaps for the best. I'm sure there were a lot of bad rumors about me. I didn't need that much negativity or distraction.

The Simple Life was a huge success, and my business was thriving. Working with Parlux Ltd., I launched my lifestyle brand and introduced my first fragrance—Paris Hilton, female and male variations—which sold so well that I decided to purchase a large home. Wendy White assisted me in locating a property on Kings Road above the Sunset Strip, which I later refurbished to add "Club Paris," the ideal after-party location, complete with an incredible sound system, full bar, and pole-dance pole.

I enjoyed selecting music and gathering people who contributed to the bizarre and amazing atmosphere of these all-night events: musicians, models, artists, actors, and a variety of other people doing outrageously exciting things with technology and media. So many new faces showed up at my door. Anna Faris recently reminded me of the night she came, starstruck and bashful, unaccustomed to a fast-paced society. I led her upstairs, and we sat in my closet, talking and laughing while I demonstrated how to do the smokey eye, which was about to become popular again.

This could be the true start of my career as a DJ, as I never stopped playing music. I navigated every gathering like a spacecraft, never leaving anyone behind. The 2004 soundtrack was typified by Outkast's double album Speakerboxxx/The Love Below and Snoop Dogg's "Drop It Like It's Hot."

That year's best films included Mean Girls, Anchorman, The Notebook, 13 Going on 30, Napoleon Dynamite, Shaun of the Dead, Howl's Moving Castle, and 50 First Dates.

Nicole and I began filming season two, which saw us driving across the country on a road trip while doing odd jobs to fund our adventure. One of the instances involved a dude ranch, which I was looking forward to. I adore horses. Despite the fact that I hadn't ridden in a long time, I felt confident. Everything began out alright, but I believe my horse was nervous because of all the foreign camera equipment and people around. He lurched forward and gained momentum. I lost my natural rhythm and began bouncing high off the saddle, so when the horse bucked and kicked, I couldn't keep up.

I struck the ground hard. My wind had been knocked out, so I lay there for a minute, straining to breathe. By the time the crew arrived, I was sitting up and repeating, "I'm okay, I'm okay." Then I felt a strange sensation like molten lava streaming down the side of my body. I had slipped into a patch of stinging nettles, which appear soft and fluffy but are actually coated in millions of tiny needles, each as fine as an eyelash and packed with acid. It felt like a spear had gone through my torso. I tried to remain in character and make it hilarious, but I was in agony. The great joke of the show was one of the cowboys offering to pee on me, which was intended to relieve the sting. No, thanks.

(FYI, that's a myth, most likely derived from an incident in which a cowboy peed himself because it hurt so terribly.)

As the show grew in popularity, the parts Nicole and I created became widely distributed. Walking down the street in New York, I could hear girls smiling and singing, "Sanasa sanasa!"" "That is hot!" caught on in the same way it did in sixth grade." After we finished season two, I trademarked the phrase. I wasn't sure what I wanted to do with it, but I knew I didn't want anyone else to arrive first.

Nicky was 19 and killing it. She showcased her high-end apparel line, Nicholai, during New York Fashion Week, as well as a range of dresses and rompers for her Chick ready-to-wear label. We collaborated with Samantha Thavasa, a Japanese luxury handbag manufacturer. Nicky designed and signed the bags, and we modeled for billboards, runways, and advertising campaigns. Every time we visited Japan, fans went crazy. It was as though the Beatles had landed. Promoters squeezed a month's worth of work into seven days.

We had a great time working as the Hilton sisters. We lived together for a while in my apartment on Kings Road, and we traveled a lot, promoting our product lines all over the world and having a great time.

That summer, I experienced a strange incident that, while not as significant as some of my other experiences, was upsetting: the first of many break-ins at my Kings Road home. Not the Bling Ring break-ins. And not the stalker with knives. Someone else. People broke into that house as if it were a Cadbury creme egg.

The building had been plundered and was clearly a crime scene. I wanted to get inside to escape the paparazzi, but the cops had it all taped off, so I went across the street and climbed over the fence at a neighboring property, which happened to be the home of my former boyfriend Jason Shaw, and I got so tangled up on the gate that the alarms went off. Cops swarmed, followed by paparazzi. It was beyond me.

Nicky said, "I'm calling Elliot."

In the 1960s and 1970s, Elliot Mintz presented Headshop, a TV discussion program where he interviewed legendary figures such as Bob Dylan, Mick Jagger, Timothy Leary, and Salvador Dalí. He was a close friend of John Lennon and Yoko Ono, and he remained by Yoko's side after John was slain. Elliot continues to be a fixture at my parents' Thanksgiving meal. He had a thorough understanding of celebrity and the media, as well as a large network of intriguing friends who trusted him, which is unusual in Hollywood. People dubbed him a "Hollywood fixer" or a "spin wizard." When asked what he does, Elliot Mintz responds, "I clean up what gets tainted and magnify what glows."

Nicky made the call, and Elliot arrived within an hour.

As he fought his way through the crowd, I observed he had no problem getting the paparazzi to behave. They were in awe of Elliot's ability, which is access. When he rolled up, they split like the Red Sea. He dealt with the cops, got me back into my house, and created a media statement that magically diverted attention away from my broken home and fence-climbing attempt and toward my developing business and new scent.

After everything was said and done, Elliot requested some food to be brought, and we sat down for a long time. I admired Jiminy Cricket's ethics and the meticulous thoughtfulness with which he spoke. Even after all these years, the one thing about Elliot that continues to impress me is his ability to think before speaking. Every syllable represents a precise footstep.

"What are your plans?He asked. "What's your wish?" Your ambition? I ask everyone of my customers, "What do you want to achieve?""

I did not lie. I replied, "I want to be famous. I want people to be aware of who I am and like me so that I may sell them goods. My product line. Nicky's product line. Designers, makers, everything I enjoy. If I say something is beautiful, they assume it must be beautiful. If I go to this club, spa, or resort, everyone wants to go too. I want people to value my viewpoint as a tastemaker. As an icon. And I'd like to commercialize that a lot."

"Your immediate presence has been established," Elliot explained. "You're past the embryonic stage of this career you're developing."

I nodded. "It's going pretty well."

"Like a runaway train," he replied. "Are you concerned about overexposure?"

"I don't believe in overexposure."

"There are parameters. There is a turnaround factor. You must be mindful when it becomes irritating.

I shrugged. Agree to disagree. For the moment. We spent a long time discussing the changing environment of media and what it means to be a celebrity.

Elliot stated, "My specialty is how much a person can do while promoting their own work, where they become secondary in that dialogue, and it's about that performance in the movie, that innovative sound they created in the music, and what was revealed in the book that changed people's lives." That, to me, is the key to excellent, long-lasting media. You can't just be about the sell. Remember, there are limited versions.

"Maybe," I said. Exclusivity. That was more of my love language.

"If you reach a smaller number of people with real potency and power, they will stay with you forever," Elliot told me.

I didn't realize it at the time, but he was describing my Little Hiltons, a rock-solid core group of followers who were like family to me in many ways.

"You have a career of forty years," he informed me. "You don't have to burn it all out in five. Artists, unlike sportsmen, have a limited number of years to be viable. There are numerous examples of artists that continue to create and inspire two or three generations of admirers after decades of superb work."

Looking for a specific method for putting all of this theory into practice, I showed him the daily torrent of media requests and messages on my phone.

"Your life," he explained, "is a whirlwind. People rarely appreciate how much time they must dedicate to maintaining their celebrity. It is a full-time, 24/7 job. When you go into Ralph's at 1 a.m., you're on. When you're sick, you're ready. When you're exhausted, you turn on."

"I know."

"When you climb a fence—"

"Elliot," I said, "I'm in on the joke."

He understood what I was talking about. And he understood why I needed him to know. That is what made Elliot an integral part of my working life for numerous years, and continues to be an indispensable part of our family now. He selected requests and helped me practice a few talking points, but more importantly, he helped me develop a philosophy that would keep me grounded in the midst of this firestorm I'd sparked. In terms of crisis management, Elliot gave me the same advice he provides to all of his clients: don't lie. Learn from Clinton and Nixon. "You're better off just admitting it and moving on."

Even when we were arguing or distracted, I knew I could contact him if I needed him.

As it turned out, I really needed him. Nicky saw this coming.

Days and weeks flew by in an endless loop: work, party, travel, party, runway, party, repeat. Elliot created an elegant proclamation for every engagement and a tender statement for each split. When my personal bullet train derailed, he gave the same clarity and calming presence that Wendy White always did. Elliot spent many nights a week with me and my friends. As the designated driver, he drank chardonnay and drove us about without judgment. Brit, Nicole, and I always called him Chardy. Nicky and I enjoyed tormenting him over the phone.

Look, I have done and spoken things that I am not proud of. I used to wear those horrible Von Dutch caps. I once attended a Playboy Mansion Halloween party dressed as Sexy Pocahontas. At eighteen, I got drunk and sang a very inappropriate version of Snoop Dogg's "Gin and Juice" at a party, and yes, I understood all of the lyrics. When I was put on the spot in an interview, I claimed to vote for Donald Trump because he was an old family friend and controlled the first modeling agency I signed with—and when I left to go to another agency, he was irate and threatened the crap out of me over the phone. The reality is considerably worse: I did not vote at all.

Do I stand by these decisions? Would I make the same decisions again, knowing what I know now? Of course, not! None of this reflects the person I am today.

People evolve. We have the ability to learn. And everyone makes mistakes when they're young. We must let go of the CEDU "dirt list" mentality and find a way to balance accountability and grace.

They don't match, but they do go together.

You wake up one morning and realize, "Wow, that was not a good look." You try to set things right. You apologize—in private when it matters, and in public if it helps. Then you move on. I'm not pretending to be the Dalai Lama wearing Louboutins here. I'm just saying that grace is available to everyone if we make it available to one another.

The Simple Life aired for five seasons. Lots of laughs. Plenty of drama. During that period, Demi Lovato had several partners, including a Backstreet Boy, a couple of Greek heirs, a bunch of hungry tigers, and what she refers to as "clout chasers."

My book, Confessions of an Heiress, landed at number seven on the New York Times bestseller list, and I toured the world, meeting hundreds of millions of people who adored my Little Hiltons. I worked in modeling, film, and television, released many fragrances, and cooperated on eyeglasses, skin care, shoes, and bags ranging from phone cases to pillow shams. Eventually, my brand extended to include retail spaces, spas, and specialized hotels.

Throughout all of this—and everything else that happened from summer 2007 to spring 2008—director-cinematographer Adria Petty followed me about with a handheld camcorder, filming an insane amount of video for a documentary titled Paris, Not France. It began as a behind-the-scenes look at the album I was working on, but Adria so beautifully captured the frenetic pace and edgy vibe of my life at the time that we looked at this incredible footage and agreed: "This isn't some DVD extra, this is a fucking film." Adria put it all together with brilliant music, smash-cut editing, and commentary from Camille Paglia, elevating the film to a discussion of what celebrity had become.

Adria got the film into festivals all over the world—Cannes, Toronto, everywhere—which terrified me because it had some information about the sex tape. And if that wasn't enough, Elliot called one day while we were filming to inform me that someone had "acquired" the contents of an old storage unit containing my personal items, such as family photos, private notebooks, and medical information. They asked me to pay a large quantity of money to have my belongings back, and if I didn't, all of these extremely sensitive documents would be released on a subscription-based website, similar to how the sex video had been.

Before I could answer, the website was up and received 1.2 million hits inside the first forty hours. People might evaluate and gossip about my private medical history, which included invoices and statements from a previous pregnancy. I guess this was the scenario when I was meant to explain a miscarriage or justify an abortion, and I said, "Fuck that." No woman, famous or not, should have to discuss her reproductive health with strangers. Denying a woman her right to privacy is a physical and psychological attack. People that do this do not want to be thought of as rapists, yet that is exactly what they are. Rape is about power, not sex. Sexualizing an assault is the most efficient way to make a woman believe that the rest of the world is judging and condemning her—which is typically the case.

I've endured it in several ways, including the man who roofied me, the orderlies who molested me, the ex who leaked the sex tape, and everyone who saw it. And this. Those folks overcame me and shackled me down with shame and humiliation that they well deserved. It took me a long time to figure it out, and I'm still working on it, but when I put the blame where it belongs—on the individuals who harmed me—they lose power, and I'm free.

Elliot arrived on his metaphorical white horse and hunted the scoundrel down. He spared me most of the details, but my understanding is that it was similar to the situation involving Pamela Anderson and Tommy Lee and their infamous sex tape back in the day: someone got hold of my private stuff and tried to sell it, and because he was a buffoon, other people stole it from him and profited from it.

The scenario dragged on for a few years until late one night, Elliot had a long come-to-Jesus chat with this guy who'd made a living promoting sleaze and blackmailing celebrities like me, Tom Cruise, and countless others. Elliot believed he'd made some progress and scheduled a meeting with the man, who appeared fatigued from his creepy life's work and really eager in seeking some type of redemption. The scandalmonger committed suicide in the shower prior to the conference.

Karma is a bitch.

CHAPTER 13

STARS ARE BLIND

The following years saw a frenzy of cutting-edge smartphones. I tested BlackBerry and Razr and maintained a couple of new flip phones in my arsenal. I organized another large launch event for the Sidekick 3 in Los Angeles, as well as another for the Razr's rollout in Japan. This technological tsunami was all about sex, color, and usefulness, transporting people easily into a completely new way of social and commercial interaction.

I was diagnosed with ADHD in my early twenties. I don't recall much of it because I didn't think it was such a huge deal. The doctor may have handed me a leaflet or something, but I don't recall him saying anything about it. He wrote a prescription for Adderall, which I took. It did help occasionally, but I despised it for a variety of reasons. (Dr. Hallowell placed me on Vyvanse in 2022, and it changed my life.)

As I learned more about how ADHD rewires the brain over time, my obsession with technology became more understandable. I was constantly moving onto the next thing. Finally, the rest of the world appeared to be catching up. It was exciting to discover tools that matched my unique rhythm—things that instantaneously reacted to the hands they were in. Apps were in development. AI was learning. I couldn't wait to get my hands on the next big thing, and I had the money to do it. With my laptop and a fast internet connection, I was never alone in my bed at night. Someone somewhere in the world was awake and doing something interesting.

Facebook became publicly available in 2006. (Thanks again to my first manager for screwing me over on that one.) Twitter had a limited start in 2006 before going viral at SXSW the next year.

Twitter was an ADHD wet dream: a constant rush of new ideas, visuals, directions, and possibilities.

At twenty-five, I was simply having fun, crying out little things that made me happy. But there was no doubting the commercial power—the direct, bankable influence—of that cheerful little shoutout. If I tweeted about a bag, shoe, or shirt that I adored, along with a link to the designer or company, sales would immediately increase. It was not an advertisement, and most of the time I was not compensated for it. I wasn't thinking about how I could control and monetize it, and I believe that is why it worked. It needed to be organic. The smartest thing I did was to continue living my life and finding it out as I went.

Meanwhile, designers and marketing trend spotters spotted what I was doing and began sending me a variety of presents, including clothing, accessories, sunglasses, dog toys, the latest technology, and even cars, in the hopes that I would write about them. Every day, UPS arrived and unloaded a ton of boxes. Every closet and spare room was packed. Faye Resnick was helping me refurbish my house and I hired Kim Kardashian to help me organize everything.

Kim had launched a business where she went into famous people's closets, stole what they didn't like, and sold it on eBay. It was brilliant and raised tens of thousands of dollars for charity and fun money. She performed an amazing job, and we had a lot of fun working together.

We counterbalanced each other. I was a disorganized night owl, but Kim was an effective early riser. It was fantastic to have someone I could trust and rely on. We traveled everywhere together, including New York, Las Vegas, Miami, Australia, Germany, and Ibiza.

The song of the summer—at least my summer—was "Stars Are Blind." For me, it will always be the ultimate beach blanket tune: a little vacation-destination reggae, a little boardwalk ska, all love and sun. Sheppard Solomon and Jimmy Iovine were working on an idea with Gwen Stefani in mind, but when Warner Bros. informed them that I had been signed to do an album, Shep said, "I have something that might be perfect." Shep filled out the song, fitting it to my voice and style, and I loved it. Shep and Fernando Garibay, who is well-known for his beats, created the song. I trusted their instincts and they trusted mine. That song resonated with every aspect of me.

It made me joyful.

You can hear it in the music.

There are no tricks or extra tech. That was the most authentic version of myself I had ever been. I stood in the booth, calm and happy, and for a brief moment, all the sadness of my adolescence vanished. The character I played on The Simple Life, who was gradually taking over my life in the real world, is nowhere to be found in this song. Each line was created with attention and precision. It improved with each minute, breath, phrase, and detail we added. I couldn't wait for everyone to hear it.

"Stars Are Blind" was released on June 5, 2006, and peaked at number 18 on the Billboard Hot 100 before taking on a life of its own. People still tell me how it characterized their summer, along with Nacho Libre, Talladega Nights, and The Devil Wears Prada. Charli XCX tweeted a few years ago, "Stars Are Blind is a pop classic" and mentioned it as a key influence. During a red carpet interview, Lady Gaga said, "?'Stars Are Blind' is one of the best pop records ever. You joke, but it would be interesting to have such a famous blond woman in the studio with me."

I'm quite proud of that music! I simply want it to last forever. I recently remastered it, inspired by Taylor Swift's takeover of her back catalog.

In 2019, I received a letter from Emerald Fennell, a writer-director, requesting permission to use "Stars Are Blind," which she had written for a critical scene in "Promising Young Woman". The movie sounded humorous but dark, and she had a brilliant idea for this song that was her "ultimate bop." She said, "I need a song that, if a boy you liked knew every word to it, you'd be incredibly impressed." If you've watched the movie, you'll understand what she means. (If you haven't seen the movie yet, then watch it now!) The scenario takes place in a drugstore. Cassie (Carey Mulligan) dances with Ryan (Bo Burnham), an old acquaintance, and their casual friendship develops right before our eyes. They fall in love in the pleasant, cheerful atmosphere of this song. Promising Young Woman is a rape vengeance drama filled with latent feminine wrath, but that moment allows us to see Cassie's baseline innocence still exists.

Promising Young Woman was made available for streaming on Christmas Day 2020. The world was in quarantine mode, so it never received the full theatrical debut it deserved. It received numerous Oscar nominations—Best Picture, Best Director, Best Actress, Best Editing, Best Original Screenplay, and the screenplay won—but I would have wanted to attend the premiere in full glory.

Instead, Carter and I watched it together in bed. We were aboard a yacht someplace over our Christmas holiday. In the pure, joyous space of that song, I allowed myself to experience my own baseline innocence—a baseline joy—that no one could ever take away from me. I adored this lovely, good man. And he adored me. I had the capacity to love and be loved. It was such a relief to finally know that about myself after years of reasonable uncertainty.

Tumblr began in 2007, and Apple unveiled the iPhone. I felt a monumental beginning, but also the end of an era for me. The Simple Life was in its final season, during which Nicole and I worked as camp counselors, and there appeared to be a shift in the party spirit. The wide-open windows of social media made it simple to go viral one day and then be devoured whole the next. People appeared and departed so rapidly that you never knew who they were. My peers and I pushed ourselves to the limit, and not everyone survived. I witnessed a lot of folks go through the meat grinder of quick stardom.

I wanted everyone to love me—I was always on, always moving, forging connections and finding opportunities to collaborate with individuals I respected. Every night, I went out with boyfriends or girlfriends, and Elliot usually accompanied us as the designated driver. But sometimes I just wanted to do my own thing. I enjoy driving, so I normally use my own car to and from work.

On September 7, 2006, I woke up around three a.m. and dozed in the chair while getting ready for the second day of a music video shoot for my song "Nothing in This World." The plot revolves around a kid who is bullied at school until I move into the house next door and accompany him to school so he can be a big man on campus. It's reminiscent of when I went to prom with the sweetest, nerdiest kid. His older sister asked Nicky to accompany him, and she refused because she had a boyfriend, but I said, "Yaasss!""I was twenty-three and still hadn't gotten over the fact that I'd never been to prom. We went through the entire process—corsage, limo, mom snapping pictures in the backyard—and when we arrived at the dance, everyone went crazy. "Is Paris fucking Hilton here? What's up with that guy?"It was one of the best nights of my life."

So, this video is very cute, but there are a lot of moving elements. We worked for approximately sixteen hours and never had time to eat, but when we finished, I joined the group to toast with a margarita. I felt OK, but on my way home, I was stopped for speeding and blew a 0.08 on the Breathalyzer, which is the absolute minimum for a DUI in California. I pulled up to the In-N-Out drive-thru, waiting for a burger and fries, which would have probably fixed the problem.

It is the least spectacular flameout in celebrity history.

Also the most expensive margarita in margarita history.

I spent the entire process feeling dumb and angry—at myself more than anyone else. It was way past midnight. I couldn't determine whether it was worse to call my parents and disrupt their sleep or to have them wake up to the news in the morning. I contacted Elliot, and he picked me up at the station house. I only wanted to go home, but I knew the media would be waiting. I offered to go to a friend's place, but Elliot responded, "You should return home. They need to see that you are completely sober.

When he arrived at the gate, I realized I wasn't in for the normal dance with the paparazzi. There was a distinct type of energy. Even through the closed car window, I could hear one of them ridiculing me in a shrill voice: "Hee hee hee hee, I'm here!""—as I waited for Elliot to come around and open the door. I walked out claiming to be on the phone.

"Paris! Paris, how are you feeling? Paris! Can you explain what happened?"

"She's not going to make any comment this early," Elliot added. "I'll come out and see you in about ten minutes."

"Okay, goodbye. "I love you," I told the imagined person on the phone. I entered the code into the gate's alarm and smiled for the cameras before entering. The boys must have been handsomely compensated for staying up late; I saw that tape repeatedly on the news the next day, followed by a quick Q&A with Elliot.

"You saw her moments ago," he told the paparazzi outside my gate. "She was obviously not inebriated. She wasn't intoxicated. However, in such a situation, the officers did what was necessary. They transported her to the station. She followed the same procedure that everyone else did. When it was found that she was clearly not a flight danger and was not intoxicated, she was released on her own recognizance."

He highlighted that I had only one drink and received no special treatment during the processing.

"Will Paris spend time detoxing?" they inquired. It appeared that was what people wanted. A big addiction/redemption sob tale, but I didn't have one, and I remembered Elliot's advice when we first met: "Don't lie. Just own it." The next morning, I contacted Ryan Seacrest and delivered a calm, straightforward interview on the radio, accepting responsibility and offering no excuses. I went to court and received three years of probation, a $1500 fine, a four-month license suspension, and court-ordered alcohol education sessions.

Okay, fair enough. I accepted it. Even if they were stretching to charge me with DUI, there were times when I was likely over the limit but didn't get caught.

Pause for an important message: DO NOT DRINK AND DRIVE.

It's dumb, hazardous, and will mess you up. Even if you don't feel inebriated, avoid going there. Also, don't text while driving for the same reason. DON'T DRIVE if you're distracted, agitated, or tired. Even though I was barely on the verge of testing positive for tipsy, I was far too fatigued to drive, and I've heard that's worse, even if it's not illegal. I deserved to be punished for making such a dumb decision.

I did not deserve what came next.

My lawyer informed me that I couldn't drive for thirty days and could only drive to and from work for the next ninety days. The day the suspension was removed (according to him), I was driving to work and was pulled up for speeding. And I didn't have my lights turned on. The city roadway was well-lit, but that idiotic mistake still hurts my head. My lawyer, who had never handled a DUI before, did not have the drive-for-work waiver he claimed to have. He informed Elliot, who informed me that I could drive as of that day, despite the fact that the papers stated otherwise. My license was completely suspended.

The lawyer threw Elliot under the bus, and Elliot blamed himself, but I was a grown lady driving around in a $50,000 automobile. It was my obligation to manage myself. I should have read the fine print in the paperwork rather than relying on others to tell me what I could and couldn't do. Even in the brilliantly illuminated roadway, I should have had my lights turned on. I earned a ticket just like everybody else. Miscommunication on the suspension escalated the situation. Now I was considering going to jail, which worried me.

My parents were heartbroken, yet they were with me. My family rallied behind me and adored me. All of the grace I could have asked for from Mom and Dad as a teenager was available to me right now. Mom could tell I was terrified, so she let me cling to her like a tiny tree frog.

Elliot attempted to testify that he had assured me it was fine for me to drive to and from work, but the judge would not have it. He was literally days away from retiring and appeared to embrace this final great event, his fifteen minutes of fame. He sentenced me to forty-five days in jail and ordered that I serve that time in county correctional—maximum security for violent offenders—rather than the "glamor slammer" for nonviolent offenders or on home arrest, as most people would in a comparable scenario. I was to set an example for all the hazardous party girls out there. The tabloids ate it up. Elliot informed me that when the judge appeared to church the following Sunday, the congregation gave him a standing ovation.

My lawyer filed an appeal, arguing that this penalty was much out of the ordinary. Elliot issued a public statement explaining what he wasn't allowed to say in court, taking it on the chin when the tabloids made it appear that I fired him in a frenzy. The truth is, I was furious with him, the lawyer, the judge, the tabloids—everyone in the goddamn world, beginning with myself.

I called Elliot the next night and we spoke for a long time. If there was ever a time when I needed him by my side, this was it. He issued another statement, claiming to be my publicist once more, and when a reporter inquired about the revolving-door turnaround, he responded the most Elliot thing I'd ever heard him say: "I don't want to revisit that which is divisive. I'm solely interested in what brings healing."

CHAPTER 14

COACHELLA

Coachella and I have a history. We both entered adulthood in 1999, struggled for a few years before finding our footing and spending the following two decades blazing in all our neon glory.

Coachella takes place every spring at the Empire Polo Club, a seventy-eight-acre field located around twenty minutes from Palm Springs. During the year I lived in Rancho Mirage with my grandmother, we spent many Saturday afternoons at Empire Polo Club, exploring the grounds and watching games. I like looking at the horses. She enjoyed looking at the men. It had a similar atmosphere to the polo scene in Pretty Woman, which was filmed in the Los Angeles Equestrian Center in Burbank but is essentially a duplicate of a regular Saturday afternoon in Coachella Valley. Gram Cracker and I were always dressed up and stylish, wearing summer skirts and ballet flats. You couldn't wear heels; it would be a painful afternoon going around on the lawn.

Coachella, officially known as the Coachella Valley Music and Arts Festival, was dubbed the "anti-Woodstock" in the early 2000s because it gave plenty of toilets, food, and water to a crowd of gorgeous people who were generally courteous and well-behaved. This new generation of festival-goers has little interest in wallowing in the mud. If you enjoy mud, I will see you at Glastonbury.

Brent Bolthouse founded the Neon Carnival in 2009, an invitation-only after-party for celebrities. He's still nailing it, and we've been together since my sweet sixteen birthday celebration at Pop in 1997. I was obsessed from the very first year. Last week, someone asked me, "Will you be attending the Neon Carnival?" I said, "Honey, I am the Neon Carnival."

I am writing this in 2022. Festival season is finally back after being killed by COVID two years in a row. I am a little concerned about my clothes. I'm usually a control freak about wardrobe for Coachella and Burning Man, obsessing over every detail months in advance, but I've been insanely busy working on a mirror event—a Neon Carnival in the metaverse—so at the last minute, I called my friend Shoddy Lynn, who owns Dolls Kill, a sick raver store that sells glitzy, Goth, artistic, crazy, sexy clothes and accessories. I enjoy supporting this woman-owned small business.

I also had Michael Costello make me a few daytime dresses that are flowing and boho chic, which I can pair with ballerina flats from Nicky's French Sole collaboration. I'll be a floaty-lace angel in the morning and a ripped-fishnet brat at night. Every outfit requires glitz and a picture session, so it must be prepared ahead of time or it will take up too much enjoyable time, which is already limited because I can only be there for one weekend. Normally, I wouldn't skip the second weekend of Coachella, but Carter has a business function that I need to attend, along with all of the other supporting spouses.

Domestic "wifey for lifey" responsibilities like those excite me in an odd way. Carter and I know how to manipulate a room as a power couple, something we both learned from our parents. I'm not sure how to define it, but it exists—this smooth, sweeping ease, an unconscious type of communication that cannot be learnt or faked. It only happens when you truly respect, trust, and support one another. Perhaps the best term for it is alliance. We're in it together. I care about what Carter cares about. Carter cares about the same things I do.

Even still, I'm concerned the FOMO will be real when I see everyone else's Coachella Weekend 2 photos.

My life has changed significantly since my last visit to Coachella. I've changed—for the better, I believe—but the most significant difference is having Carter with me. The first few years of our relationship coincided with quarantine. This marks our first festival season together. Carter is standing in the foyer, astounded by the amount of luggage I require for a three-day weekend: two dozen suitcases and garment bags, multiple bins containing bags, crowns, sunglasses, several cases of glam and tech equipment, and a life-size cardboard cutout of DJ Paul "Let's get Fizzy!" Fisher, founder of Fizz hard seltzer. Everything makes sense. Trust me.

I don't give it much thought, but Coachella is an excellent illustration of how my ADHD view of time applies to trend spotting: In Spirograph's view, I walk the polo field with Gram Cracker and attend the Neon Carnival with Carter. I feel the ground beneath my strong boots and lovely ballet flats. If the proper influencer says the best of all worlds is a gorgeous platform boot, someone—preferably a tiny, woman-owned business—will sell a lot of them.

We load out and leave before daylight, flying to Palm Springs in a private plane, and then settling into our home-base hotel suite, where my staff assists me in reorganizing everything in a walk-in closet. Friday morning, we drove up behind Coachella's main stage in a Greyhound bus-sized RV. In the next 72 hours, I only get around 10 hours of true sleep. I would get even less if I didn't sleep while having my hair and makeup done.

Marilyn Monroe used to do the same thing: lie there sleeping while the glam team worked as if they were applying cosmetics on a corpse. It isn't excellent quality sleep. More of a power nap. I'm fine with it for the weekend. It's kind of exciting to wake up with iridescent lips and Sailor Moon space hairstyles, and I need to make the most of my one weekend at Coachella.

First and foremost is the music. Between mainstage acts—Megan Thee Stallion, Harry Styles, Billie Eilish, Swedish House Mafia with The Weeknd, and Doja Cat—there's a steady cycle of incredible talent on eight stages. I have to plan a timetable and actually dash from one stage to the next in my platform boots, making sure I have time for all of my favorite DJ performances and—my favorite—the Neon Carnival.

The Neon Carnival is the last vestige of the LA party scene we adored at the turn of the century.

"New York had Studio 54," Brent told me recently, "but we had the 1990s and 2000s. "You could go to a club in Los Angeles on a Monday night and it felt like an Emmy party."

I'm not the only one who still wants to celebrate like it's 1999.

The Neon Carnival is a customized event that reminds me of those enormously entertaining, bright turn-of-the-century celebrations. It was originally hosted within a massive airplane hangar, but after 10 years, it was relocated to the HITS (Horse Shows in the Sun) Equestrian Center. The guest list is limited. There are no tables or tickets for sale. It doesn't matter whether you have money or a large Instagram following.

There are celebrities like me and venture capitalists like Carter, but celebrity and money aren't the only things that matter. A skater poet from Venice, a race-car driver from Australia, models from Japan, advertising moguls from Kenya, people from different cultures, people with different abilities, loud people, quiet people, straight people, gay people, drag queens, drama queens, introverted extroverts, and extroverted introverts are all equally likely to meet. The only thing we have in common is that we're alive and glowing with milky neon splendor.

For Neon Carnival, avant-garde fashion is the norm rather than the exception, so the outfits, hair, and makeup are out of control, but not as expensive or difficult to move around in as the avant-garde looks seen at the VMAs and the Met Gala. I enjoy seeing people deviate from the norm and exhibit their own freakiness, whatever it may be. I think I'll wear a little black dress with neon green beads that come alive in black light, plus sunglasses from my new Quay collab, a fleecy neon rainbow bomber jacket from Dolls Kill, and a little hologram backpack for my phones, ketchup packets (Heinz and fries, always), extra tiaras (designed by Melissa Loschy of Loschy Crowns, who makes these glorious bespoke headpieces and sells them on Etsy) so I can gift them as the spirit moves me, a couple of fragrances Because it is hot. Temperature-wise.

Following the 2008 economic crash, the internet became more democratized through Web 2.0. We began discussing the "long tail" concept of creator material that went beyond the box. No more product launch windows. No more gatekeepers. You can now build and direct your own marketing campaigns from the palm of your hand. I was on the cutting edge of it all, with all the name recognition—for better or worse—powering my platform, which led to some fantastic possibilities in film, television, and traditional media.

Some others argued that the old and new worlds were irreconcilable, but I saw it as a healthy symbiotic combination. There was no clear path for me to follow, and no role models to learn from. I simply stretched my wings, and the updraft took me.

During the 2008 presidential election, the McCain team bizarrely opted to utilize photographs of me in their advertisements to represent the worst thing they could think of: a "Hollywood celebrity." I suppose their purpose was to equate Barack Obama with me and Brit—vacuous celebrities with nothing to add to the conversation. A new website called Funny or Die approached me with a wonderful concept, and I created a series of "Paris for President" faux campaign ads that have some of my favorite lines ever.

Instagram and Pinterest were first established in 2010. The major films were Inception and The Social Network. The party atmosphere was obviously changing now that you knew that whatever you did, wherever you went, someone had a camera, and whatever you said or did might be broadcast to the entire globe in seconds. Casey Johnson died only a few days into the new year. She'd been best friends with Nicky and me since we were tiny children, and the last photographs I saw on Instagram showed her beaming with joy. Wearing a shimmering gold mini with snakeskin shoes and a Chanel handbag. I clicked the small heart. It was unbelievable that Nicky and I would never see her again.

In 2011, I turned thirty. It marked a new era for social media as an art form. Twitter quickly gained popularity, followed by Instagram, and I was among the first to join. I saw it as an opportunity to grow my global brand. Along with the possibility to further my personal interests, I sought opportunities to support people and causes I believed in.

I tried out for a new reality show with Mom, The World According to Paris, some of which was filmed during my community service hours following a small possession bust. There was no major deal there, just a small bit of marijuana, which is legal now and should have been legal then—especially for those suffering from PTSD—but it wasn't, so it was a fair shake. I completed my 200 hours of service, and we had such much fun that I added another 350 hours. I was pleased that we were able to draw attention to deserving groups that serve the homeless in LA.

The play was enjoyable, and Mom was wonderful. Because travel controlled my life, I decided to launch a Passport Collection of fragrances—Paris, South Beach, Tokyo, and St. Moritz—and tour the world to promote them. I sponsored a motorcycle team in Madrid and walked at Brazil Fashion Week while Lady Gaga's "Born This Way" played in the backdrop. I had a lot of fun writing about my travels on Twitter until I realized that when you write about all the great locations you're visiting, people notice you're not at home and rob you.

I was shocked to discover that a group of high school kids later known as the "Bling Ring" had entered my home on multiple occasions while I was away, stealing jewelry, shoes, clothes, cash, and whatever else they desired. I know it's difficult to feel sorry for someone whose closet is so overflowing that they don't instantly notice a million dollars' worth of missing items, but when I eventually got home and realized what had occurred, I felt violated and enraged.

I had worked so hard for this space. I was fatigued when I arrived home. This was meant to be my shelter. It took me a long time to feel safe there again, but I couldn't bear the thought of leaving. I was done running away. Anyway, this house was very amazing. Sofia Coppola asked me whether she could shoot The Bling Ring here.

"There's no way to recreate it," she explained. "It has to be the real thing."

It was therapeutic to transform what had transpired into a wonderful work of art. I adore Emma Watson and the entire cast. The crew was aware that this was a real home in which a real person lived her life.

My life, company, and brand were all about embracing your "hot" appearance, living in beautiful homes with attractive stuff and adorable pets, and hanging out with girls who know how to have fun. I grew up in the most chaotic moment of popular culture since Cleopatra. Everything felt like it was moving too quickly. Runways, parties, appearances, skiing, skydiving, cuddly pets, beautiful people, iconic photo shoots, sisterhood, business, fragrances, family, fans, nightclubs, lashes, bags, redefining femininity, creating music, putting beauty in the eye of the beholder, making art an experience and experiencing art as a way of life—there's a lot. I understand. I'm fine with extra.

The Little Hiltons and I altered what it meant to be famous. More importantly, we redefined what it meant to be yourself.

CHAPTER 15

AMNESIA

Amnesia is the place I go to forget. Whatever you're trying to leave behind, believe me, it can't compete with the amazing excitement of this arena-sized club in the heart of Ibiza, a Mediterranean island between Spain and North Africa.

I first heard about this institution when I was fifteen years old and living with my family at the Waldorf. I begged my father to let me go there, but he spoke with the concierge, who responded, "No, no, no." Not Ibiza. This is a notorious party island. "This is not the place for good girls to go."

So no Ibiza for me till I was old enough and had earned enough money to travel there on my own.

In 2006, I planned an extraordinary female trip for myself, Caroline D'Amore, and Kim Kardashian. We remained in a tent beside my buddy Jade Jagger's house. It was quite boho and hip. Kim wasn't a big clubber in general, and neither of us had ever had an experience like Amnesia. The super clubs don't open until the bars surrounding the island perimeter are about to close, so the celebration doesn't even begin until 3:00 a.m. Most people come to dance and enjoy the music, not to drink. Kim and I were wise and watched out for one another. Reliable backup is a crucial part of the girlfriend's journey. The relentless music is too loud to hear anyone calling out, so gather a group of trusted party mates and keep an eye on each other.

Amnesia's production qualities were really high. Unbelievable sound systems. Epic laser light shows illuminate the crowd. Music pulsing with a special type of house style—the Balearic beat, a distinct sound originating in those islands. We were up in a VIP position with a fantastic view of the booth, where the DJ was handling a complex array of turntables and mixers. This was the first time I paid close attention to what the DJ was doing and realized how effective it was. Killing it like a rockstar, he commanded the entire room with thousands of people in his palm.

They then fired the foam cannons.

The dress code prohibits shorts, T-shirts, and flip-flops, although most people wore swimsuits underneath their clothes. I took off my party dress, tied it around my waist, and continued dancing in my bikini.

"Paris! Come here!" The foam girls motioned me over to the fence.

I took control of the cannon and sprayed lemon-scented foam all over the audience below. People went berserk, bouncing around like rubber duckies in a bubble bath. Kim and I couldn't quit laughing. Our faces lit up with the same delight that you see when tiny kids tumble down a waterslide. That exhilarating happiness was what I hoped people would feel when they attended the Foam and Diamonds party I presented at Amnesia for five years. I wanted them to depart like we did: weary and elated, blinking in the early morning sun.

I wanted to return to the hotel and sleep, but Kim wanted to enjoy daytime life in Ibiza, so we went to the beach and slept on the white sand.

Kim covered her eyes with her arm and chuckled. "That was lit."

"That DJ's hot," I said. "One day I'm going to be up there."

"A girl can dream."

"The Secret states that life does not happen to you. You are generating it, and I am going to build it."

"You and The Secret," Kim remarked. "You're obsessed."

"For real, though."

"I believe in you." She was half asleep, but she seemed serious.

I answered, "I believe in you, too, babe."

The water was chilly and vividly blue. Caroline and I were floating on inflatable rafts, exhausted after dancing all night, when we fell asleep and woke half a mile offshore.

Years passed before I began DJing, but this is when it all came together. I was still in my teens when I found I could get paid to attend parties, and I learnt a lot while attending the top parties and clubs throughout the world. People would come to see celebrities, but only a superb DJ could deliver the exhilarating experience we witnessed in Ibiza that night. I knew if I put in the effort to master the technology, I would be able to accomplish both.

The first thing I discovered was that it's much more difficult than it appears, but I'm smart enough to ask questions rather than pretend to know everything. A fantastic guy named Mike Henderson, nicknamed DJ Endo, taught me the fundamentals of hardware and software. Over the next few years, in between doing a million other things, I spent hundreds of hours learning all there was to know about DJing, teaching myself all the tricks I could find on YouTube, and developing a few new ones of my own. I attended every major festival, including Burning Man, Coachella, Ultra, and Tomorrowland, to observe, absorb, and feel the energy, as well as understand how to keep people jumping and raging.

I encountered some knee-jerk pushback, as would any woman in an extremely male-dominated business. When I first started doing gigs, several people refused to accept it was me. I couldn't make room in my mind for that. I worked harder, proved myself, and moved forward. I booked huge music festivals and megaclubs in the United States, China, Europe, and the Middle East. Finally, I made it back to Ibiza.

During my five-year tenure at Amnesia, family, friends, and thousands of fans—so many of my Little Hiltons—came from all over the world, and it was just what I had hoped for. It was difficult for me to set aside several weeks each summer, so I knew the closing party in 2017 would be my last vacation to Ibiza for a while. I enjoyed it there, but business was booming.

My fragrances had generated about $3 billion in revenue, and I was working on nineteen additional lifestyle brands such as skin care, shoes, clothing, purses, lipstick, lighting, home décor, pet fashions, and whatever else I could think of off a mood board. My real estate holdings included spas and nightclubs, and I even followed in my great-grandfather's footsteps by opening my own hotels. I was writing and recording music, and I was always willing to film a movie or make an appearance in the appropriate location for the right cash.

For twenty years, when every inch of my skin was exposed to the public, I kept some things secret. The effort left me lean and distant, tough enough to withstand mind-bending success, soul-crushing betrayals, and staggering volumes of my own nonsense.

But eventually, everyone leaves Ibiza.

Amnesia was never long enough for me. No matter how hard I worked or played, I had to sleep at some point, and my nightmares reminded me. It was as if my experience in jail unlocked a cellar door that I had kept locked for a long time. The dreams had never left me, but spending twenty-three days in jail intensified them. It became real again. Immediate. Physical. Dangerous. I didn't just wake up screaming; I was battling for air, as if I were trapped at the bottom of a muddy river.

Sometimes I got up and brought my laptop into bed with me. It was an unhealthy habit. The first time I looked up "Provo Canyon School," I was astounded to discover that it still existed. After so many years. Nobody had done anything about it. This includes me. The remorse felt like the sting of a wasp. Because this is what pedophiles, abusers, and rapists do: they make you complicit in their crimes by providing you with the one thing that threatens them: now you know. You could stop them. If you do nothing, you'll be responsible for the next one. Of course, this is all nonsense, unfair, and false, but I know I'm not the only one who has carried that load. Many survivors have told their memories and grieved with me, both of us filled with sorrow for every child who suffered while we struggled to flee that place. Our sanity—sometimes even our survival—depended on forgetting that location and building a life in which we'd never have to think about it again.

With the rise of Reddit and other communities, survivors of Provo and CEDU began to piece together a horrific history of abandonment and abuse. The scale of the devastation was heartbreaking: addiction, PTSD, suicide, disrupted sleep, and broken families. And there was so much money that it stole my breath away. These facilities received billions of dollars in private and public support. It was so filthy bad that they kept changing company companies to avoid litigation and allegations. CEDU Education was sold to Brown Schools in 1998. They declared bankruptcy in 2005 and were acquired by United Health Service, Inc. They vanished and reappeared, like Whac-A-Mole. Some attempts had been made to hold them accountable, but no one was able to lay blame on them.

I had to look away. I had to reassure myself, "This is not my fault." There is nothing I can do. I couldn't take part in this. What if someone from one of these boards remembered me? Have you disliked me in the past? All that rap crap. The kangaroo kicks. The entire stabbing scheme was blamed on me. My brand was more than just my business; it represented my identity, strength, self-esteem, independence, and entire life. I needed to defend my brand. Anything off-brand—no. Create a slash-shaped circle. I can't have that.

I returned to my secure haven: work.

In 2012, Facebook acquired Instagram, while Twitter acquired Vine. I started an eyewear business in Shanghai and traveled with my sixteenth fragrance, Dazzle, which is still one of my favorites and provided a reprieve from the Spanish model I was dating. I had entered into a franchise agreement that included forty Paris Hilton retail outlets, largely in Europe and Asia, offering handbags, skin care, sunglasses, and other branded items.

In 2013 and 2014, when I wasn't doing DJ residencies in Atlantic City and Ibiza or doing performances in Spain, France, Portugal, South Korea, and the United States, I was in the studio creating my own music. Along with my traditional theme music, I added two new singles, "High Off My Love" and "Come Alive," to my performance. More than ever, I felt Ultra Naté's "Free."

I couldn't get rid of the image of the children being imprisoned at Provo Canyon institution, but I felt exactly how the institution had taught me to feel: impotent.

I wanted to help, but I didn't know who to contact. Anything I did would jeopardize my carefully prepared narrative. It meant potentially harming or shaming my family.

I felt protective of Papa. He was robust for his age, but when Nanu died in 2004, he lost some of his spark. He was never an emotional guy, but as I developed into my life as a businesswoman, we found a lot in common. That bond was significant to me. In 2014, I pursued my real estate ambitions, opening Paris Beach Club in the Philippines, and he was all for it. When I brought him out to dinner,

I'd ask him if he wanted to go out the back to avoid the cameras, but he was proud and pleased to take my arm and walk out the front.

It meant a lot to me to see my parents so pleased with what I had done. I won Best Female DJ at the NRJ DJ Awards, and Time magazine said I was the highest-paid female DJ in the industry, earning up to a million dollars every gig. I'm still working toward the day when we can remove the "female" from that debate. There are so many amazing female DJs out there now that the word feels out of date and out of place. Opportunities abound; the boys have nothing to be afraid of. If you are good, you will find work. Competition is beneficial, right?

Nicky was also killing it. Her book, 365 Style, was published, and she became engaged to James Rothschild, who was both magnificent and Rothschild.

All of this is to imply that I did not want to upset the family by bringing up terrible memories from the past.

In 2015, "High Off My Love" peaked at #3 on the Billboard club chart, I performed to a crowd of 50,000 at Summerfest in Milwaukee, and Nicky married James at Kensington Palace. The low point was losing Tinkerbell, my faithful friend through so many highs and lows. She died of old age at fourteen.

TikTok, which began in 2016, became an instant sensation. Donald Trump was elected president. And I became an aunt when Nicky and James welcomed their beautiful daughter, Lily-Grace Victoria. Her younger sister, Theodora Marilyn, was born in 2017.

Being Aunt Paris brings out a new level of fierceness in me. As I watched these magnificent little creatures grow, memories of my own early childhood surfaced in the back of my mind. I was once a happy, free-spirited little mermaid of a child. And then. ..Something happened.

TikTok and Instagram made it simple for me to pretend my life was a flawless fairy tale, but in reality, my fairy tale life did not occur: elite prep school, Ivy League college, graduate studies abroad, a career in animal science, a nice husband, and children. All that vanished before I could even conceive it. Now I was trapped within the Simple Life caricature, this me-but-not-really-person who was out there living my life.

Social networking has become the new reality.

Selfies were created.

Privacy became commodified.

Our collective attention span has become ad space.

Ritalin numbed an entire generation of youngsters, but they somehow reinvented the art of connection.

I felt carried by a wave of empowerment. It surged up beneath me as women of all ages became dissatisfied with the way we had been dismissed. Now I was working hard to shed my skin and leave behind the baby-voiced character. I aspired to be the woman Marilyn never had a chance to become: It Girl turned Influencer.

Everything I do is based on rapidly evolving technology: music, social media, DJing, visual arts, product development and design, NFTs, and whatever comes next. Carter and I discussed a lot about how we'll raise our children in the midst of it.

(We talk a lot about kids in general since we're excited to have them one day.)

"I can't imagine what it means to be a thirteen-year-old girl in this day and age," I told myself. "We'll have to be strict about screen time."

"Our parents faced the same difficulty," Carter explained, "but they had to be tough about computer usage and video games. And their parents had to be tough about this new invention called television."

Isn't it mind-blowing? It's all happening so quickly.

But I had a brick wall built around me. I worked hard to keep it there. Made some awful decisions. Allowing some damaging impacts. I wasted so much time with hungry hangers-on and attractive bullies who always appeared to require money, constant attention, or both. If I happened to meet a man who was man enough, I would always find a way to ruin things.

"I don't feel that bad for you," Nicky said after I broke up with someone I can barely remember. "If you wanted children and a husband, you'd figure out how to make it happen. Perhaps you don't want it. You believe society expects this of you, yet it is a great burden. If you don't really want it, don't do it."

I wanted it. Genuinely! But there was a part of me that wasn't ready for the kind of collaboration I saw between Papa and Nanu, Mom and Dad, and now Nicholas and James. I accepted that it was not something I was capable of. I couldn't imagine myself ever unlearning that old lesson: I'm better off on my own.

I traveled 250 days each year. My time was taken up with creation and cultivation. Make things happen. It was my lifeblood. And all of this activity protected me from memory. Every gig, flight, and photo session, as well as every cameo role and throwaway boyfriend, contributed to the wall I created around me. Nobody knows me better than Nicky. The fact that I never informed her what actually happened when I was apparently "away at boarding school in London" demonstrates how completely I buried it.

I reached thirty-six in 2017, the same age as Marilyn Monroe and Princess Diana when they died. Whatever route they blazed for me stopped here. Something weird needs to happen to make me feel settled.

Reality TV proposals were a constant in my life, and I generally declined without attending the meeting. I did not want to go backward. But I kept hearing from Aaron Saidman, the executive producer of the documentary Leah Remini: Scientology and the Aftermath. I was impressed by the level of homework he completed and the substance he was aiming for.

At our first meeting, Aaron informed me, "I went down a rabbit hole by reading a lot of news. A lot of it was unflattering. Critical. I began to consider who would be reading all of those pieces. We spent twenty years obsessing over Paris Hilton and speaking about the Hilton sisters, but you were not talking about yourself. We were all having that conversation, but every time a scandal emerged, the family would circle the wagons. They dispatched a public relations representative to handle the criticism."

I had to smile when I thought about Elliot enjoying his chardonnay.

I clean up what is soiled and enhance what shines.

The scariest part of the entire procedure was sitting down with my mother and telling her what had really transpired. Looking at her face, I saw disbelief, then shock, and finally genuine sadness. All the times I sobbed for her—so many scary nights and miserable days when my heart kept wailing, "Mom, mom, mom," it's as if she heard everything at once. Overwhelmed, she covered her face with her hands, pressing her fingers against her forehead for an extended period of silence. When she looked up again, her face was calm and beautiful. A mask of grace under strain. She had to deal with it in her own manner.

At first, I assumed she was still the queen of sweeping things under the rug, but a few days later, I received a text from her with a link to an article on Provo Canyon survivors, as if she wanted me to know she was ready to dive down the rabbit hole. We then had a slow, deliberate discourse about the past, being mindful of each other's sentiments and not wanting to add to the sorrow.

As my advocacy work grows, I'm focused on urgently needed legislation to protect children still in custody, but I'm also acutely aware of the families torn apart by the troubled-teen industry—families that begin in crisis and end up completely dismembered, with crippling debt and deep, deep emotional scars. They need assistance as well. They require healing.

Having my mother with me on legislative action trips gives me hope for those families. Privately, we haven't gone over everything. I'm not sure if we ever will. Her willingness to discuss it publicly demonstrates remarkable fortitude. Her presence conveys a simple yet powerful message: Mom is here.

CHAPTER 16

THIS IS PARIS

Carter likes to say he cured me of my clubitis, which I suppose is another term for FOMO. And my fear of missing out was extreme. I kept going year after year, feeling compelled to make up for lost time.

The carousel ride continued around and around, following the same global itinerary year after year: the Cannes Film Festival. Let's go. After Cannes, there's the Monaco Grand Prix. From there, we fly to Ibiza, Saint-Tropez, Tomorrowland, Coachella, Burning Man, Ultra Music Festival, Art Basel, Miami, and EDC. There was a complete program of must-see events, including red carpets, film premieres, and spectacular after-parties. I remodeled my new home with plenty of closet space, a recording studio, and an updated, grown-up version of Club Paris, where I convened with my friends whenever I was home.

Carter and I crossed paths frequently during those years. He attended many of the same festivals and events, and he tells me that he, his brother Courtney, and cousin Jay crashed several parties at my place. I didn't invite them—I didn't even know them—but we had so many friends in common that they fit right in. Jay appears to have spent the evening smoking weed with Snoop Dogg and Suge Knight in an upstairs room. He returned to Michigan and told everyone about it, and it became one of the family's favorite stories: "That Time Jay Got Stoned with Snoop and Suge."

Carter's family always gathers over the holidays. He grew up in a little hamlet outside of Chicago. I adore the fact that he is from the Midwest. After college, he worked for Goldman Sachs until he and Courtney relocated to Los Angeles to launch VEEV, a high-end alcohol brand—one of the fastest-growing private firms in the US—and established their venture capital firm, M13 Investments, in 2016.

He likes to believe we knew one another because we were in the same place at the same time numerous times, but the truth is that I didn't see him. I was too busy being the Queen of the Night. I attended Burning Man in August 2019, when This Is Paris was still in post production. Carter was present when a friend stopped by to say hello and take a quick photo. I looked straight through him.

It's odd. Perhaps we were meant for each other, but God didn't let me see him until I was prepared.

In the fall, holiday preparations began to form, and Mom invited me to the Hamptons for Thanksgiving with family and friends. This was something I hadn't done in almost fifteen years. I have always worked. I always had a cause to be somewhere other than the dinner table with my parents, whether it was London, India, or anywhere else. That was a tough no for me, especially when I learned Nicky and James were traveling to Abu Dhabi.

"I'm not sitting there alone with Mom and Dad," I told them. "That would be incredibly lame."

"Paris," Nicky replied in a demanding, little sister voice, "go see your family." Don't become an orphan. The females will be there. You haven't seen Lily Grace or Teddi in a while, and they're growing so quickly."

I told her I'd think about it, and as I looked around Los Angeles, I realized I was weary of being detached and wandering, of attending parties where I had to play a predetermined role.

I felt ready to go home.

Thanksgiving week was filled with cooking, eating, and socializing. Mom was asked to dinner at a friend's place, and she invited me to join her. She expected me to make an explanation about wanting sleep or go shopping, but I simply answered, "Sure."

I anticipated being bored out of my mind, but when I arrived and saw this cute guy—tall and athletic with an amazing grin and kind eyes—I thought, Okay, this could be interesting. Halle, Carter's sister, is married to the son of my mother's friend. Carter's father had died unexpectedly two years before, therefore Carter was accompanied only by his mother, Sherry, a petite steel-magnolia lady. Carter's care for her was very sweet: attentive but not overbearing, empathetic but firm. He always kept her in the corner of his eye.

When Carter spotted me, his face brightened up. Carter claims that when he noticed me sitting by the fire with a cup of hot chocolate, he told his brother to run interference so he could chat to me alone for a while. We went over the standard hello and how are you questions, and I realized this guy assumed I knew who he was. He mentioned Burning Man, and I tried to be friendly, saying, "Oh, yeah. "Of course." He inquired about my impending plans, and I responded, "I'm supposed to go on this trip with the Dalai Lama and a bunch of other people."

He replied, "Oh, I know some guys going on that trip. Let me have your phone number so I can introduce you." He did not know anyone on the trip. It was only a workaround to get my real phone number without appearing unduly demanding.

When guests began to gather for dinner, I went to the powder room to refresh, and Carter went to the table, seating his mother on his left and bogarting the chair on his right to keep it available for me. When I sat next to him, he made no attempt to be cool about it. He was just ecstatic to be sitting with me. As the evening progressed, we discussed families, art, life, business, and our mutual favorite subject: work. Carter kept talking about work while I sat there trying to figure out how to get him outdoors so I could kiss him.

One of the servers leaned in and said gently, "Miss Hilton, I see you aren't eating. "Is there anything else we can get you?"

"No," I replied. "I don't like to eat in front of cute boys."

After dinner, I asked him if he wanted to take for a walk outside and essentially jumped him. I pushed him up against the tennis court barrier and kissed him, after which we made out like teenagers for ten to fifteen minutes.

Carter replied, "Well. "I wasn't expecting that."

"I get what I want," declared the Queen of the Night.

"I should get going," Carter said. "We're going back into the city tonight. I'm staying at the Plaza with my mother and brother."

I was thinking, "Wait—what?" Is that it? Then they left.

Google emergency. I spent the rest of the night investigating this guy, looking into his company, and seeing him on YouTube conducting interviews and business analysis for CBS, Fox, and Hatched, a show about entrepreneurs.

He was so darn cute. I was obsessed. I needed to see him again.

"Don't go to the city," Mom said. "You'll look desperate."

And I felt desperate. I stayed one more night in the Hamptons, got up, and packed my belongings. I told Mom, "I have to see him."

I returned to my flat in New York. Carter came over. We ordered Mr. Chow's, drank a bottle of wine, and spoke for hours. I told him about the upcoming documentary, which would unveil a stunning fact to the public. He listened to my narrative with tears in his eyes.

For the first time in my life, I started a relationship on the basis of complete disclosure. I made a connection that did not involve distinct nooks for closely guarded secrets. We were honest with one another. Isn't it a crazy concept? First and foremost, you own it. Then you can share it.

My walls collapsed quietly and totally.

Carter and I spent a lot of time together over the course of the next few months. I created room for it, made it a priority, by declining every request to go dancing or jet-setting. My friends kept asking if I was okay, and I replied, "I am fine. I just don't want to ruin it with this great person."

A few months later, in March 2020, the COVID pandemic shut everything down, and my boisterous world was silent. I couldn't recall the last time I spent so many days at home. This was something I had always imagined would drive me insane. But I enjoyed it. Carter and I disappeared into our own universe. We cooked, cleaned, and took care of one another. He was compassionate with my recently opened heart. This was a new experience for me: a truly mature relationship with a man who is my equal. He brought back the joy I felt as a child and made me feel ready to have my own children.

We knew it was forever. We knew we were a family. We began IVF with big aspirations about our adorable brood and the life we'd create around them.

Quarantine was a welcome respite for Carter and me, but the rising death toll was scary. So many of my fans have experienced loss and tragedy. Many of the individuals we love were particularly vulnerable. I felt bad for being so blessed and fortunate in the midst of such sorrow.

I was sorry for Alexandra when the This Is Paris premiere was canceled, but it felt like compassion to me. I was pleased that it arrived at that critical period of required refuge. I was unsure how it would be appreciated by the general public or, more importantly, my family. There was no way to forecast how it would impact every aspect of my professional and personal life.

This Is Paris was posted on YouTube on September 14, 2020, and it received over sixteen million views in the first thirty days. The instant impact was more than I could have imagined, yet it was difficult for my family to finally face the truth about what had happened. Healing is a continuing process, as is likely the case in every family.

Since the release of This Is Paris, I've made several trips to Washington, DC, to meet with politicians and White House staff about the critically needed revisions in legislation governing regulation and oversight of the disastrous teen industry. With Carter's full support, I hired impact producer Rebecca Mellinger. Her roles include turning outrage into action, such as organizing rallies and news conferences, managing position papers, and hosting our podcast Trapped in Treatment with Caroline Cole, a survivor of the troubled-teen industry. Rebecca and I completed a legislative-action training course, which opened my eyes to how much power we—as in We the People—truly possess. My goal is to close down any facility with a history of abuse and ensure that every child has access to adequate care.

We want kids in therapy to know that we are here for them.

And we want institutional abusers to know that we're coming for them.

The bills and laws we helped enact are my career's crowning achievement, and I am most proud of them. I wish Papa, Nanu, and Gram Cracker were here to witness this. I kind of wish Conrad Hilton was here to see it! And it gives me awful pleasure to know that the individuals who harmed me and so many other children can see it. I hope they are terrified.

I finally showed up—for myself and someone else—and it feels incredible. I sleep at night knowing I'm doing everything I can to help children caught up in a web of lies, abuse, and silence.

Carter has been very supportive of my attempts to raise awareness and effect serious change in the troubled adolescent industry. He adores the fact that I am a warrior woman, an activist, and a creator tycoon who works on a mood board or goes over profit and loss statements while he works on a product pipeline or acquisitions paperwork. I can honestly state that no man has ever loved me for the reasons Carter does. I had no idea that being in a relationship could make you feel both safe and empowered.

In February 2021, I appeared before a Senate subcommittee, encouraging them to pass Senate Bill 127, which was later passed by the House of Representatives and required the Department of Health and Human Services to regulate and oversee adolescent facilities. Two weeks later, on my fortieth birthday, Carter proposed to me, and I accepted.

Our beautiful 11/11 wedding was (of course) recorded in the Peacock series Paris in Love, so I won't go into too much detail here. The program discusses all of the chaos that went into wedding planning, as well as the tremendous success we made with advocacy and a few baby steps forward in my relationship with my mother during that time. The wedding was three days of pure pleasure. The guest list was limited due to the pandemic's lingering effects, but Carter and I were surrounded by love and joy.

We've been married for three years and are content with our relationship. We enjoy going to the farmers' market on Saturday mornings to get fresh eggs, fruit, and vegetables to cook an elegant breakfast, and then we sit and eat and talk about wonderfully geeky topics like cross-collateralization and negative pickup. We laugh a lot and take time to reflect and be grateful. We enjoy our careers, our houses, and our dogs.

The Hilton pets have their own social media platform and have been in numerous commercials. Diamond Baby captured the spotlight in a series of Hilton advertising. Carter and I joke about Slivington's refusal to lift his leg for less than a quarter million. In addition to being their stage mother, I'm juggling product lines, expanding my media empire and metaverse universe, and keeping a busy calendar of events. The possibilities that come my way on a regular basis are so exceptional that I struggle to say no, but I'm learning. Carter and I both understand that money is a lot of fun, but time is the most valuable natural resource we have.

I had given it a lot of thought. Having my infant with me at work, on the road, and backstage at Fashion Week. That is the world we now live in, and it has the potential to be lovely if you can overcome the intrusive thoughts. If you can hope. And continue walking.

If all goes as planned, Carter and I will have a baby boy by the time you read this. We intend to name him Phoenix, a name I chose years ago while browsing cities, countries, and states on a map for something to go with Paris and London. Phoenix has a few nice pop culture references, but more importantly, it's the bird that burns up and then rises from the ashes to fly again. I want my son to grow up knowing that calamity and triumph repeat themselves throughout our lives, and that this should offer us enormous optimism for the future, even when the past is painful and the present appears to be trash. It's strange how two beliefs so different—so diametrically opposed—can live, but they can.

Freedom and suffering.

Joy and despair.

Love and loss.

I waited in the darkness, shoulders back, chin down, and center, until it was my turn to walk into the light.

The director did not lie. The beat was quite hot.

The contents of this book may not be copied, reproduced or transmitted without the express written permission of the author or publisher. Under no circumstances will the publisher or author be responsible or liable for any damages, compensation or monetary loss arising from the information contained in this book, whether directly or indirectly. .

Disclaimer Notice:

Although the author and publisher have made every effort to ensure the accuracy and completeness of the content, they do not, however, make any representations or warranties as to the accuracy, completeness, or reliability of the content. , suitability or availability of the information, products, services or related graphics contained in the book for any purpose. Readers are solely responsible for their use of the information contained in this book

Every effort has been made to make this book possible. If any omission or error has occurred unintentionally, the author and publisher will be happy to acknowledge it in upcoming versions.

Copyright © 2024

All rights reserved.

Printed in Great Britain
by Amazon